UNDER BERLIN
NEW POEMS 1988

John Tranter was born in Cooma, New South Wales, and grew up on an isolated farm. He has worked in teaching, printing, publishing and radio production, and has been awarded a number of fellowships from the Literary Arts Board of the Australia Council. He has travelled widely, living at various times in Sydney, Melbourne, Brisbane, London and Singapore, and lecturing and reading his poems in the United States, Canada, England, Sweden and Germany. In 1979 he edited *The New Australian Poetry*, an influential anthology that gathered some of the more experimental work of his own generation.

By the same author:

Poetry

Parallax
Red Movie
The Blast Area
The Alphabet Murders
Crying in Early Infancy
Dazed in the Ladies Lounge
Selected Poems (1982)

Anthology

The New Australian Poetry

UNDER BERLIN
NEW POEMS 1988

by

JOHN TRANTER

University of Queensland Press
ST LUCIA • LONDON • NEW YORK

First published 1988 by University of Queensland Press
Box 42, St Lucia, Queensland, Australia

© John Tranter, 1988

Designed and typeset by Lyn Tranter at Pavilion Press Set
2 Buckland Street, Broadway NSW 2007 Australia

Printed in Australia by
The Australian Print Group, Maryborough

Distributed in the UK and Europe by
University of Queensland Press
Dunhams Lane, Letchworth, Herts. SG6 1LF England

Distributed in the USA and Canada by
University of Queensland Press
250 Commercial Street, Manchester, NH 03101 USA

Creative program assisted by
the Literary Arts Board of the Australia
Council, the Federal Government's arts
funding and advisory body

Cataloguing in Publication Data

National Library of Australia

Tranter, John, 1943–   .
   Under Berlin.
   I. Title.
A821'.3

British Library (data available)

Library of Congress (applied for)

ISBN 0 7022 2137 6

For my daughter Kirsten

It is alleged by a friend of my family that I used to suffer from insomnia at the age of four; and that when she asked me how I managed to occupy my time at night I answered, 'I lie awake and think about the past.'

Ronald Knox (1888—1957)

What does the wind do? It
bothers the air.
What does the blue Pacific
do all the day long?
Makes waves, perfectly.
Why does the wino
drink to kill time? Why,
because he's a drinker.
Well, here I am, writing. So
go, little book, et
cetera.

Contents

I would like to thank the Literature Board (now the Literary Arts Board) of the Australia Council for its valuable support over many years, which directly enabled many of these poems to be written.

I would also like to thank the English Department of the Australian National University, the School of Humanities and Social Science at the New South Wales Institute of Technology, and the Department of English and Linguistics at Macquarie University for their hospitality and support during the times I spent with them as writer-in-residence.

I would also like to thank the Literature Board of the Australia Council and the Cultural Relations Section of the Department of Foreign Affairs for assistance with reading tours of the US, Canada and Europe, ventures which widened my own perspectives and enriched my writing practice, as well as helping to present Australian poetry to an appreciative audience overseas.

J.T.
Sydney, 1988

Individual poems in this book are dedicated as follows:

Californian Poppies for August Kleinzahler
Cicada Gambit for Martin Johnston
The Guides in memory of my brother Peter Hellier
Having Completed my Fortieth Year for Peter Porter
Lufthansa for Katharina Kaever
Parallel Lines for Duncan Ellis
South Coast After Rain, 1960 for Delena
The Subtitles for Jane Howard
Voodoo for John Forbes

Acknowledgments

Acknowledgment is made to the following publications, in which some of the poems in this book originally appeared:

The Adelaide Review: 'On Looking Into The American Anthology'; *Agenda* (UK): 'Lagonda', 'Shadow Boxing', 'South Coast After Rain, 1960', 'Voodoo' (then titled 'Lingua Franca'); *Ambit* (UK): 'Glow-boys'; *The Australian:* 'Creature from the Black Lagoon', 'Laminex', 'Lufthansa', 'Moonie', 'The Latin Motto'; *Helix:* 'Lagonda', 'Shadow Boxing'; *Hermes* (1986): 'Braille', 'Lullaby'; *Kunapipi* (Denmark): 'On Looking Into The American Anthology'; *London Review of Books:* 'Shadow Detail', *Meanjin:* 'Debbie & Co.', 'Dirty Weekend', 'Fine Arts', 'Glow-boys', 'Halothane', 'Having Completed My Fortieth Year', 'High School Confidential', 'Letter to America', 'Plaza Suite'; *The Melbourne Age:* 'Braille', 'Lullaby'; *The Melbourne Age Monthly Review:* 'Sail Away'; *Ninth Decade* (UK): 'During the War'; *Phoenix Review:* 'Braille', 'Voodoo'; *Poetry Review* (UK): 'Spark'; *Scripsi:* 'Bathyscape', 'Cabin Fever', 'Cruising Height', 'Parallel Lines', the sequence 'Sex Chemistry' ('Crosstalk' and 'Poolside' separately), 'Those Gods Made Permanent'; *Southerly:* 'During the War', 'Spark'; *Surfers Paradise:* 'Voodoo' (then titled 'Lingua Franca'); *The Sydney Morning Herald:* 'The Guides'; *The Times Literary Supplement* (UK): 'Country Veranda'; *Verse* (UK): 'Braille', 'Having Completed My Fortieth Year', 'High School Confidential', 'Laminex', 'Luck' (from 'Plaza Suite').

'The Subtitles' was adapted for radio, produced by Jane Howard, and broadcast by the Australian Broadcasting Corporation in September, 1985. It has since been broadcast in a French translation by La Societe National de Radiodiffusion France-Culture. 'Backyard' and 'Glow-boys' were broadcast on the Australian Broadcasting Corporation's 'A First Hearing' program. 'Lufthansa' won *The Australian* twentieth anniversary poetry prize in 1984 and was published in 1985 in the Angus & Robertson anthology of entries to that competition.

BACKYARD

The God of Smoke listens idly in the heat
    to the barbecue sausages
speaking the language of rain deceitfully
    as their fat dances.

Azure, hazed, the huge drifting sky shelters
    its threatening weather.
A screen door slams, and the kids come tumbling
    out of their arguments,

and the barrage of shouting begins, concerning
    young Sandra and Scott
and the broken badminton racquet and net
    and the burning meat.

Is that a fifties home movie, or the real
    thing? Heavens, how
a child and a beach ball in natural colour
    can break your heart.

And the brown dog worries the khaki grass
    to stop it from growing
in place of his worship, the burying bone.
    The bone that stinks.

Turn now to the God of this tattered arena
    watching over the rites
of passage — marriage, separation; adolescence
    and troubled maturity:

having served under that bright sky you may look up
    but don't ask too much:
some cold beer, a few old friends in the afternoon,
    a Southerly Buster at dusk.

COUNTRY VERANDA

1 — *Dry Weather*

This country veranda's a box for storing the sky —
      slopes, acres of air
      bleached and adrift there.

From outside, a shade-filled stage, from inside
      a quiet cinema, empty
      but for the rustling view

where a parrot scribbles a crooked scrawl of crayon
      and off-stage a crow
      laments his loneliness

and six neat magpies, relaxed but quite soon
      off to a General Meeting
      stroll, chortle and yarn.

When the summer sun cracks the thermometer, laze
      there in a deck chair,
      shake out the paper

and relax with the local news: who won the cake
      in the Ambulance raffle;
      what the Council did

about the gravel concession down at the creek, who
      suffered a nasty fall
      but should be well in a week.

2 — Rain

From that open room where sheets hang out to dry —
    cool, wet pages
    whose verses evaporate —

you stare out at the trees semaphoring their sophistry:
    their tangled, pointless plots
    and obsessive paraphernalia,

drenched among the spacious palaces of vertical rain
    where no phone rings
    and neighbors are distant.

Behind that ridge of mist and blowing eucalypt tops
    the world waited once:
    exotic, inexhaustible.

You've been there now, and found that it's not much fun.
    On the veranda, silence
    fills the long afternoon.

THE POOL

1

The pool looks up at the sun,
    and so it should,
so it should look up,
    shouts the mad sun.

2

Under the thundery summer sky
    chlorine has the scent of
pure greed, like brother and sister
    fighting over pocket money.

3

The perfect pool is bright,
    but it has no colour —
that is, its true colour
    is never spoken of.

4

Better barbecue beside it,
    in the Roman manner;
better drink pink gin
    and tumble into it.

5

Rain pimples the surface of the
    pale [undecipherable] water
in the pool made famous
    by the poet Apollonius.

6

The priests patiently explained
    the shape of the pool
to the Emperor, under the waves
    of advancing bombers.

7

This blue lingo, that
    golden dialectic
paints the bottom of the pool,
    the moving ripples.

THE BEDROOM MIRRORS

1

An alarm clock plots its
opportunity to shock. Spare
personalities droop among
moths in the upright grave.

Here is the mask-testing
apparatus, and a portrait
locked inside the glass
mouthing something important.

Outside the curtain, sunlight
seems to be struggling. Soon
the house is empty again.
The two mirrors in the room

stare at what they've been given:
a wall, a bathrobe hanging crooked,
a towel in a heap, a double bed
unmade, different each day.

Their duty is to listen.
At noon, in the blue heat,
a squeal of brakes a block away,
then the wailing that follows.

They hear the quarrelling traffic
and the planes passing overhead, then
forget what they have seen
and heard, recording nothing.

2

These upright sheets of light
show a planet whose photographs
were flopped by a careless printer.
Here, the plausible aliens dress

with their watches on the wrong
wrist; their shirts are buttoned
differently, but always, in the glass,
freshly pressed before the party.

What happens afterwards —
stains, crumpled embarrassment —
passes without comment. But
tableaux have taken place within

the jurisdiction of the mirrors
that never should have happened:
the sobbing child breaking a toy
that belonged to a special friend;

an old woman dying on the floor;
a wife naked with another man.
If you lived here, the mirrors
whisper, you'd know everything.

Would you want that? Could you,
with your weepy, weak addictions,
take in everything that happens here,
then — not a word said — let it pass?

NORTH LIGHT

He looks around his son's room: the bed
unmade, the globe of the world with an
imaginary voyage plotted in blue ink,
the clutter of books and plastic toys,
a life gathering its tackle together and
pushing forward. He stares at the backyard
and the thick bushes growing upwards.
The only movement is the glitter of leaves,
and the washing his wife hung out,
before she went to work, flapping
in its circus. Something you can't see
holds it all together. What is it? Last
spring they painted the house: amateurs,
but doing the job as best they could, then
they laid bricks in a pattern in the yard —
what is it, that makes the pattern hold?
That party where they squabbled, the dinner
where old friends got drunk and happy . . .

He sits at the kitchen table, half dressed,
drinking a glass of orange juice,
and wonders about the delicate adhesive
that holds it all together. Once, long ago,
he'd been divorced: a sad, frightened drunk
living in a rented room.
                 When the washing's dry
he'll gather it up, in armfuls, and bring it in.
He turns on some music. The house has a
northerly aspect; it is full of light.

WIDOWER

Moving among the dull red glow, which
stands for the darkness behind the eyelids,
he drifts like a sleeper, deftly making dreams
manifest. A brief beam of ghost-blue,

then the developer, rippling. This alchemy
to which his once magnificently complicated
life has shrunk, has filled his daylight hours
with its chromed gadgets and protocols.

In the evening, in the secret room scented
with expensive chemicals, he conjures up his
darlings again: a girl with hair the colour
of the tassel on the corn-cob she's holding;

and his wife — so young, in her fifties frock —
waving from an old red sportster that somehow
looks brand new. He stares and
stares, his face swollen with longing.

In the rest of the house one or two lights
have been left on, as though a family
were sitting up late, talking, or perhaps
listening to the radio, together.

SOUTH COAST AFTER RAIN, 1960

1

The clouds have drifted back to the hills
and the late afternoon sun spills onto the town
lighting up a steeple and a sign advertising
        diesel fuel.

2

In a back paddock two men
are loading a pile of drums
slowly onto an old green truck.

3

A car hurries along the road
in the distance — you can just hear it —
a teenager driving his dad's new Holden
to meet the prettiest girl in town.

4

Nightfall: the lights go on
outside the picture theatre. A gang of boys
hang around the Red Rose Café
        smoking cigarettes.

They watch a car pass
and turn at the end of the street
where the bridge points over the black water
towards the future. They watch it
        drive back.

5

Ah, the girl, how lovely she is;
at sixteen, how grown up.
He thinks of meeting her in twenty minutes,
    nothing else.

The radio glows in the dashboard,
the rock'n'roll sounds brand new.
Things will be like this
    forever.

6

I see them meet,
they fight, they separate,
travel,
        grow old.

7

The truck door slams.
One of the men opens a cold bottle.
Outside the cinema the weeds push up
    through the footpath.

8

Parked in the darkened driveway
they sink into a kiss.
                    The radio
fills the car with emotion.

PLAZA SUITE

1 — *Luck*

Her hands are quite small, each
finger slender, that recently
dawdled over the alphabet or
hammered out arguments. Yesterday

she was a little absent-minded, he
remembers, her skin cool in the room's
dusk, answering his fingertips
with a hesitant, wavering braille.

He's lucky, so far, knowing
nothing yet about a decision
she's come to at last: another
room, a different man, et cetera.

2 — Breath

When I was a kid we kept two brown
draft horses in the barn. When
a draft horse kicks you in the stomach
you don't feel a thing — that is,
there's a smacking sound, and the light
gets brighter for a moment. It's
unnerving, just how long it takes
for the rest to arrive, shaped as a
hollow, a lack, a crippling question
your kneeling body strains to deal with
in vain, silly child, in vain.

In the ash-tray, a butt touched with
sticky pink. Far below, the ridiculous
ambitions of the traffic, and above
a sky decorated with aircraft.

Old fool, why did it take you forty years
to remember the quick brightness, and
the thing that announces itself as a
hollow, a lack that reaches out to
grip you, a question your breathless
body seems quite unable to answer?

PLAZA SUITE

3 — Sammy's Song

Well, I'm finally sick of it, getting
fucked over by women — 'Jesus, you're
so . . . romantic, aren't you?' she says.
As if it's a *neurosis* or something!

I had a few roses sent up, that's all.
And okay, I burst into tears, but
after she'd left the room, and
that makes the difference, right?

I'm not a kid any more, I know how to
hold things back, when they hurt; it
shows the adult touch, respect for the
feelings of others, i.e. the fairer sex.

So she noticed I'm a little overweight —
did she have to harp on it like that?
I'm fed up with getting my heart skewered
on those Country & Western lyrics —

I'll ask that young number out tonight,
the typist with the vague blue eyes.
Oh God, I could really fall for her.
But no flowers, ever again. Fun,

fun for Number One, and a bright
smile as the lady lowers herself
into the taxi to the airport and
kisses my fingertips and waves goodbye.

I have no magic answer, just a flair
for the merry-go-round, my grip more
certain with each experience, surely. And
deep breathing, a belief in a higher form

of rational enjoyment — I'm sick of it, that
other stuff, the blurring vision . . . You know,
for all her cruelty she taught me a lesson:
a stronger person is beginning to emerge.

CROCODILE RAG

Hearing your song again on the radio
late at night reminded me to write my
schoolgirl fan letter at long last,
but your boy-friend's face in the photo
you sent, that pale flesh, made me
hate you for what you'd turned into —
please don't *tell* me those things.
I see your groupies throwing up,
sick with disappointment at the door.

You're right — your husband has a role:
literature's dentist. And if we disregard
two land masses and the South American
novelists, he's the seventeenth-
most-important person of his type
this side of the Equator. Honest.
He looks like a plump young Cary Grant,
when you make him cry, and you do that,
don't you — teasing like a piranha.

I feel confused and hostile about
my position as a recent house guest.
He was hanging about in the hallway
when your drunken party friends broke in
just as we were making love on the rug,
but I guess you wouldn't remember that.
Whatever the emotions you may have wished
to convey then, sweetheart — tenderness,
migraine, whatever — you blew it. Sorry.

Are you going to settle down now, like a
good wife? Your reputation can only
decline if the attacks get worse.
And they will. I know I'm capable of
wicked things — I'm not a Nice Girl —
but I loved you once. Now your
'Crocodile Rag' frightens me, frankly.
It's in the fingering, the heavy chords.

But hearing your voice last night
on the radio, hoarse with sorrow
brought it all back. Maybe — why not? —
we could try it one more time.

DEBBIE & Co.

The Council Pool's chockablock
with Greek kids shouting in Italian.
Isn't it Sunday afternoon?
Half the school's there, screaming,
skylarking, and bombing the deep end.
Nicky picks up her Nikon
and takes it all in, the racket
and the glare. Debbie strikes a pose.

In a patch of shade a grubby brat
dabbles ice-cream into the cement.
Tracey and Chris are missing,
mucking about behind the dressing sheds,
Nicky guesses. Who cares?
Debbie takes a dive. Emerging like a
porpoise at the edge of the pool
she finds a ledge, a covered gutter,
awash with bubbles and chlorine's
chemical gossip. Debbie yells there,
and the rude words echo.
The piss-tinted water slaps the tiles.

Debbie dries off, lights a smoke,
and gazes at her friends fading out
around the corner of a dull relationship
and disappearing.
              Under the democratic sun
her future drifts in and out of focus —
Tracey, Nicky, Chris, the whole arena
sinking into silence. Yet this is almost
Paradise: the Coke, the takeaway pizza,
a packet of Camels, Nicky's dark glasses
reflecting the way the light glitters on
anything wet. Debbie's tan needs
touching up. She lies back and dozes
on a terry-towelling print of Donald Duck.

She remembers how Brett was such a
dreamboat, until he turned into
somebody's boring husband. Tracey
reappears, looking radiant. Nicky
browses through an Adult Magazine.
Debbie goes to sleep.

MOONIE

She leaves the Marriage Lecture, shaking, late
one Friday afternoon and hits the street
with her lipstick and her plastic mask intact.
I'm in a rock band, a midget shrieks
from his playpen, but she's cruising by now
out past the limits of disprin and domestic trauma.
A coffee with a stranger, and her mind snaps.
The mongol population of the cheap bar smile
in a chorus, smiling to themselves,
listening to Satan as a talkback announcer
who really cares. You undead, about to die badly,
don't bother me now with your rotten proverbs.
I'm engaged in a group healing seminar
that runs till dawn, recycling dreams
that nobody wants. I'll cry if I want to,
won't I? Under the lights? And be a total person
with a tic, collecting dollars in the parking lot.
There's my Mom, years back, washing up,
imagining the fifties will go on forever.
One day, in the desert, a swarm of awful
things will take place, one after the other,
and I can feel the damage coming, a train
crashing through an empty station
that was left to the weather long ago.
The broken cup, why not smash it?
It's a painful journey down the brain-stem
but over the horizon something ultimate
awaits me: the Devil, a Chinaman with acne
or a family kidnapping. God has his plans.

VOODOO

From his rushing-away, from his
ever-receding throne, under a rainy
canopy of trees and scraps of cloud
that topple back, shrink and disappear,
embalmed behind his rear window in a nest of
crushed velvet plush, the flash wog's nodding dog
blinks out his witless approval to the vehicles
that shadow him forever.

His twin the dipping bird sips and sips,
tilts back, cools off, dries out,
dries out utterly, totters weakly
on the lip of philosophy
then dips again.

These two critics teach us how to live,
rehearsing the gap between the no-no
and the drink-again. Their motto? Every day
I will get better at embroidering the lingo
of the tongue-tied doctors of letters; every night,
in the lack of light, I will get better
and better at the negative virtues, telling
girls to piss off, who needs them,
swimming off the edge of the rock
ledge into the plunging broth of deeper waters,
soaring up to the stratosphere, bothering the angels
and yarning with God. My left hand does it,
my right hand tells me that it's right.

In the pre-dawn rack and bash of winter peak hour
traffic on the Sydney Harbour Bridge you notice them
hefted up over the city like ju-ju dolls
in the trance of a terrible gift. You note
the man with gauntlets and the goggled girl
on motorbikes, the nurses' giggles

in the fogged-up Mini Moke, an ambulance weaving
and howling in the rear-view mirror, the tablets
rattling in the Emergency Bucket, the icy rain
furious and seething on the road, and Noddy
and his loopy brother brooding on it all
for our sake, so that we can see it whole.

THE GUIDES

They used to be cheap and monochrome, explaining
how all Sydney was a target for the Jap subs. Like
rock'n'roll they started out in black-and-white,
    then stated the obvious —

that the Harbour was always blue, the parks army green,
and the stop lights were spreading in a scattered rash
out past the paddocks pocked by tussocks and riddled
    with pylons and power lines.

They grow a little each year, sprawling beyond
hectares of raw housing estates with extravagant names
bedecked with Bretts and Brendas and pramfuls of young
    Deborahs and Darrens.

When I was pushing at adulthood, on the painful side
of twenty, one took me to my father's funeral
in a blond building of brick in a strange suburb
    I never wanted to see

then guided me back to my city friends. Our journeys then
were measured in miles, we spoke the Queen's English
but shouted jazz in American every night above the
    living rumble of traffic.

They're brothers, Robinson and Gregory, but you never
see them together much, except in the newsagent's.
One of them's always going somewhere in a car. They say
    life's an open book.

FINE ARTS

Beyond their exhausting vanity and their hatreds
the Old Masters agreed in the small hours:
a work of art, they said, collectively,
     lies in a kind of mud:

gossip, bad faith, someone else's
wife, phone bills, a little happiness. And so we
go on, they said, doing what we can; while
across a horizon full of exasperating detail
     a headache piles up.

And yet the swimming pools are full of children
laughing in that deafening sun, and the barbecue
gets assembled. In the long afternoon one marries,
     one plans a divorce.

Are the Old Men right to maunder, taking young love
as a sketch for heaven on earth? The hot spring
fevers burn away the bossy mannerisms, bringing
complex couplings: some in beds, some on the telephone,
but mostly delirious: is this possible?
     Is that right?

An emotion as perfect as a painting hangs over Sydney,
Learn Greek in a Week can happen to a lucky student:
in the shadowy cave an apprentice, humming quietly,
colours in a background of traffic
while the Master stares through the bright doorway
     lost in the visible world.

BATHYSCAPE

As we drift up past the mug shots
and the shelving stacked with
cans of *film noir*, the fumes
of 'arts for art's sake' fill
the cabin. There's cheap alcohol
and free movies for the crew, and
Polaroid situations, developing slowly.

Over there an old couple are trying to
jog and smile at the same time.
Should we tell them acts like that
just don't cut the mustard
here in the South Pacific?

The nostalgia machine brings in the
coloured money, repeating its single trick
again and again, as the old lady yells:
'With a haircut like mine, a girl
is stuck with a string of blind dates!'
Hubby shakes a cocktail, and we take a deep
breath and break the surface.
                          That's funny —
down here in the Garment District
it's raining heavily, and the streets
are completely deserted.

CABIN FEVER

After the dinner dance, the Young Rotarians
are putting on a guessing competition and
guess what — you're it! No, I'm kidding,
Christ, cut it out, will you, Karen?
Give her one of those Relaxatabs.
Honestly, the way she picked up
the kitchen knife . . . are you kids having
a good time? You like the fairy lights?
Let's say we're all involved in a serious
political discussion, and you notice
that the host has spilled — umm —
a Grape Soda all over his lap, do you
mention it to your hostess?

                    Uh-oh, forget it,
she's lying there whacked out, staring up
at the globe covered with little mirrors
rotating slowly, the beams of light
splashing off her amethyst choker. Look,
let's forget about the dance, I just
wanted to see you again.
I've been stuck here all winter
with no one to talk to but the kangaroos.
I want to get a good look at you
with your pants off — No,
not you, lamebrain. Slip this
piece of paper to the band-leader,
will you? And meet me outside,
we'll share a cold beer and
you can tell me what they mean, these
circulating couples, these proposals.

SHADOW BOXING

Behind the canvas, see the mad painter
sparring in the cul-de-sac of his
self-regard. See the glib Professor
    weeping in the square.

We ruin the tourist ruins, eroding their
attack by the way we stare through them, or
the faster we drive the younger we grow
    until the fuel boils,

clearing the sky completely. So this is
happiness, our double greed burning the edge
of someone else's longing. Sweetheart,
    book me a couple of tickets,

I want to be elsewhere tomorrow, on a veranda
with you, thunder brilliant in the heavens,
our gentlest movements universally valid
    and the envy of angels.

CRUISING HEIGHT

The party's empty — furnished with enough drunks,
maybe, but Dick's in a pressure chamber
surfacing from some private trench: train-sick,
bombed out, he hears the sound of a crowd
raving around its lack of focus.
Now he tips backwards through layers
of some muscle-paralysing gas that causes
sweating, as the girl gets a drink — a Fuel Tank,
vodka and ice — then warm, technicolored,
more keenly balanced than an autopilot
switching back to manual she gives him
the perfect present of a smile.

                            As the random
self-absorption of a tranquilliser acts like
the secret paint that soaks up Russian radar,
so, locked in this casual chat, he becomes
invisible, and tracks her monologue the way
petrol-scented dawn hunts down a westbound jet,
the molten gold reluctant to unpaint the fuselage
as they lift, sun and craft together — reading
the way her smile clicks on a fraction too eagerly
to mean a downtown version of the rocket shot
group grin as the green lights blink awake
and in slow motion the launch window
tumbles up to the horizon.

                        A crush
in the front seat and Richard retranslates
the four seasons: Autumn, refrigerator
pump repair, a Winter of television interference,
Spring as a blizzard of hormones and Summer
sliding across the surface of our discourse
with ourselves like a Lounge Lizard.

Dick, are you okay? No, he's still submerged,
but struggling heartily, and as he reaches for
a fresh emotion he sees the school of years
drifting into oblivion and the night sky
like a blanket lit with glow-worms.
Beam me up, Scottie! He's a jet
jockey. Switching on, he hears the engine
kick into life, and feels the planet turning
imperceptibly beneath an orange moon.

BRAILLE

It's a job — teaching half-blind adolescents
complex and fascinating lies. As you
flip open the textbook a photograph
of someone oddly familiar
leaps off the page — yes, it's you,
though disguised awkwardly, and the subject
of a damaging attack. Look, there —
the career you took so long to build lies
crushed and broken like a truck in a compacter:
now you'll have to teach that too.
While your self-respect is convalescing
they keep you busy gluing up the cracks
in the one-way mirror with a two-part adhesive.
And outside, clearing the lawn of debris,
you can see yourself reflected in the silverfoil
that covers the glass walls of this asylum
and somehow paints it blue. Much later,
in the Bar, your drink dissolves its ice-block
shaped like Australia while a young student
stares hard at her gift, a mouth painting —
that's how long she takes
to make a wish, crossing her fingers
and poking her tongue out, but it's only art,
and the 'Portrait of Teacher
With a White Cane' lies doggo. Galloping
for the goal-posts at the end of your mind
your need to kiss her collides head-on with your
image of yourself — you see sparks, then
everything's just like it used to be, only
more so — deft as handwriting in italic.
Believing in it makes it real,
you tell her; and she does.

THE CREATURE FROM THE BLACK LAGOON

Sunbathing on deck's the done thing,
but it makes the Brylcreem run
and stain the collar of your poplin
beach shirt. Palm trees drift by
as though your sins had turned vegetable
and semaphore. Sins of the laboratory, I mean,
not the confessional . . . yes, the engine room
looks suitable, and through the porthole
a wise old man waiting patiently
in the wavering water — that's no priest!
Captain! But the Captain's a yellow
foreigner, drinks gin, and never shaves.
You pity the girl in the bathing suit —
she may be a palaeontologist, but
sure as eggs she's going to get
a terrible fright. And the ethnics,
they have to die on our journey
towards the knowledge that shimmers behind
the South American facade. The priest
turns his scaly back: that creature,
rising like a new disease from the gene pool,
why should we pity him? Deracinated,
maybe, but what a guy! No, it's wrong,
don't kiss him! I can feel it,
soaking through the blood-brain barrier . . .
he's never known the touch of a woman's . . . whoops!
Here's the nut with the speargun on a hunting
spree — Duck, Tabby! Duck and cover! Here comes
the bolt from the blue, to shut up sorrow,
to stop up the barrel of fun like a dead
king.
      And what colour's the blood, Doctor? Red?
Can you explain that? And what of the offspring?

SPARK

Before that war we lost, our obligations
were enamelled around the inside-out horizon
of a Boy Scout biscuit tin, and Dad
deciphered them by pointing with his pipe.
'Boarding school ruined their manhood,' he grunted.
'Look at Suez, look at the King who stuttered!

We took the Costa del Dago from the grip of Foreigners,
now sit on it!' I will, I am. 'Write "The rose gardens
full of bank managers," write "The bodies
of collaborators piled high against the wall." '
Drop a German bomber from a wreath of secrets
in the boiling purple cloud, Father. Can do.

'The boffins here are Sympathisers — faggots —
watch me quaff a beaker foaming with a yellow
poison gas I knocked up this morning! But
I'm wearing out a welcome,' Dad said, peering
at the blue spark chasing itself around the rim
of the charge accumulator. 'Killer voltage, what!'

I'm spelling out a halo, or a counterfeit thanks
tossed on the zinc to blink and catch the sun.
I scribble 'Pissed on Spanish plonk!'
I inscribe 'Cable lots of money, soonest,
dearest!' and chuckle. Oh the flesh, so pallid,
of the clerks from Bognor Regis! The negro

sailors strolling languidly under the trees,
their kisses like the touch of burning metal!
'A spin in the dented Bentley with the chap from MI5
and the war was practically over. Dead Jerries,'
Dad ventured, 'Damn their sick and heady music!
Roses blooming all the summer long. Write!' Will do.

1

Remember blotting paper? The Year of the Pen?
Pen, I mean, not roller-ball. Come on, gang —
you guys — applied to girls — those teenagers,
they seem to have disappeared, behind
a fit of the giggles, or a hot flush.
One minute they're practising the drawback,
confusing innocence with ignorance, then
you look into the glass and they're all gone.
Did they just fade out, bathed in the glow
from a fifties movie? Did the girls all wear
plaid? And pony-tails? Hey Butch,
let's have a pillow fight . . . outside,
a snowfall blankets the small town.
The crew-cuts, the red and green
checkered shirts adorn Dad's jalopy
bumping away from the zone of focus
like insignia stencilling a boundary
around their tribe and epoch.

2

TV holds some fascinating specimens, sure thing,
an endless museum that seems stranger and less
human the more we gaze at it through the faint
reflection, glazed on the screen,
that reminds us of someone important,
though it seems to play possum: one face
layered on the other, related somehow,
across a mysterious dimension that never moves
yet through which all things move
towards a common grave.

STRATOCRUISER

This is a dream I had each night in Korea,
where I was very busy killing in a plane:
I boarded an ocean liner as my destiny
ordered, and sailed away. The sun came up
over the scented tropics, day after day.
Then the underbelly of Europe appeared:
its black ice, its suffocating manners.

And then I was nodding off in the bar
downstairs in the Stratocruiser —
endless thunder over the Sea of Japan,
droning home through a mile-high wall of rain —
you wake up just as you think 'touchdown',
and the fat tyres kiss the wet tarmac, bump,
shriek, and touch again.

           The flak jacket
waiting to be invented, your shabby suit
hanging at the cleaners with another name
carefully printed on the tag — your roles
were there all along, shifting slightly
in the shadows of a doorway somewhere in
South-east Asia, but still yours, and you
slip back into the last half of the century,
unannounced, unmarked, without a second look.

GLOW-BOYS

Four a.m. At the reactor an alarm begins
howling. The core's full of shit: get out
the gloves, the phosphorescent rakes.
A burnt-out star hangs low on the horizon.
The Harrisburg glow-boys knuckle down
to work, poking around in the ashes.
They gaze out through glitter: behind the visor
putty imitates a human face, the lips
gritty, frayed, as they reach for speech
across the static field. Now a bell rings
and they wade thigh-deep into the muck,
their eyes the colour of lightning.
Five years of that and they're
too hot to touch; they wake screaming
before dawn, the pillow soaked.
What have they seen: their children's future
flare and crackle, a vast Christmas tree
flashing up from the skyline?
Rake it up, Ratshit! In a month
vacation in the Rockies, drinking rye and
blowing rattlesnakes away with a shotgun.
Now, like any cleaners, they go to work
deft and grumbling, their wives awake
in nylon nighties staring at the ceiling
and the glow of the luminous clock.
The pot of coffee popping on the stove.
The kids asleep, dreaming fitfully.

LETTER TO AMERICA

1

Those guys cranking up the price
of admission to Paradise,

they're soap powder, all froth and bubble,
or a hair dryer, hot air.

Our gang's a laundromat, doing things
at regular intervals.

And soon we sketch the circuit board the ideal
mind dreams of —

chatty, smooth, like a template
of a stunning quiz show,

or a wheel spinning, the way the spokes
almost meet at the hub,

that's good, each conscious of his own job, then
they rush out to the rim

where they flash and glitter, kiss
the speeding dirt. Almost

2

I hear an old drunk colliding
with a stack of bottles, I hear
a maniac whisper in the dim kennel
to the dogs of war, spittle on his chin.
That sad dark age, the honour rotting, is it
as black as we imagine, or as permanent?
A lick of orange light from a neon
paints a chrome grille in your room —
the monitor ticking, everything aware —
history is shifting hugely, a mountain pushed by
a hundred million taxpayers, a shift discernible
but only just, and then at the periphery,
the edge of the screen, in the detail
of an alcoholic beaten in an alley,
the price of groceries climbing . . .
Can you see these pictures? Projected
blurring on a wall? Staring through the tears . . .
There, those teenagers, laughing on the pier,
the hot dogs, it's unendurable — the Thunderbird
that caught alight, havoc in the air,
a childhood perjured for a bitter drink
that unhhh . . . led me here, dammit,
to the dark side of democracy, the drowning pool
among the bodies tangled in the rusted autos —
alone at last, stripped of the right to vote.

3

Those robot ants are building a language
with a rapid assembly overlay — it might be tight
and vicious, but it fits the bill. Ah,
beyond the acres of hatred there's a map
that gives you nearly everything!
There's a good degree, there's a photograph
of naked women eating money, there's
a bomb designer who could be a close
friend, given the time and the motive.
Looking west from New York you can see
a glow on the horizon: it's NORAD
gearing up for the night shift, a shuffling
under the Rockies as the workers wake up
and start packing lunches. Up above, the radar
nets rotate, catching star whispers and planes
packed with drugs flaking up from Mexico.
Down the rough, uneven slope to the Pacific
the dialects break in through the static —
threats, promises, the sound of dollar bills.
Kids wake up in small towns wide-eyed
and stare out at the pools of lamplight
on the grass — they feel a shudder in the stomach,
something tugs at them, a hypnosis ray
out of *Popular Mechanics*, but an alien
hand's on the throttle. Sex, and killing people,
they didn't teach this in the gym, and so
their tomboy dreams are troubled by the sound
of distant engines coughing into life.
Further west the reaches of the ocean. Then the moon

4

A house hidden behind a screen of brush
at the end of the Korean War and the
dawn of rock'n'roll plays host to a feast
of sick movies that he calls The Daily Planet.
The computer gives him light in the darkened
kitchen; with a faint whining noise a flash unit
recycles beside the folding camera.
He pads through the house, gathering evidence.
He had four good wheels, he had
gasoline singing in back of his head.
Hey Harry, how do you stop this thing?
He still ached from the divorce.
Park and Lock your ethics here,
a sign on his retina said, beneath this
building that's a mirror for the wreckage.
Fear sketching in the blank faces as the diary
fills up with missed business opportunities.
How come their lies are rewarded with a
gift of strength that doubles on itself?
Knock a few wetbacks into the gutter
that runs the length of Sunset to the sea.
Then a pina colada in Rudi's: after
the spilling glare of the Strip
it was a relief to come across a lobby
filled with geriatrics doing nothing.
In the ideal ecological niche, he realised,
everybody has a bolt-hole, or a buddy
in adversity. Was that right?
Then a take-away in a motel room, watching
the Table Talk Chicken Thighs
cool at the side of the bed.
Then the bad dreams.

ON LOOKING INTO
THE AMERICAN ANTHOLOGY

1

In California a young man is stuffing a briefcase —
first a jug of light, the words 'water'
and 'stone', a blurred image of a guy in a pickup
    truck with a gun

staring through the hush-squeak, hush-squeak
of the wipers, a frail woman, crying. A leaf, a sob,
a clod of mud. There! His class awaits the real,
    the Deep and Meaningful.

Driving downtown he sees a pair of jugglers
inch up the face of a glass cathedral full of
marriages, mirrored in the noon glare, one on top,
    and then his double.

The neon signs in the suburbs full of graves say
'Giants Drank and Died Here'. Autos, rusting trucks,
police helicopters roam restlessly, their motto: Do it
    First, and Do it Fast.

2

Down here in New Zealand, jet-lagged in transit
at the bottom of the planet, a clutch of
Flight Attendants giggle in a corner: one gay,
   the others married.

The sun that has looked down on Hollywood,
on lust, Las Vegas and the will to power,
rises, *rhododactylos*, on Auckland Airport:
   through the tinted glass

a perfect field of fodder, five sheep,
a tractor nosing at the sedge, the shrill
cacophony of jets rehearsing like a madman
   staring at a vase.

Nothing the amusing natives do here matters
in the Capital. The giant engines lift us
through the sky. The next stop — Australia —
   is the end of the line.

LAMINEX

Staring through the steam that clouds the window
of Abdul's Pizza Bar on King Street, you reconstruct
Newtown — the Newtown of the rag trade avant-garde —
as the heat ripples rebuild the traffic.
The teenage dreamers cruising their torpor
for a cheap hit mean less and less as
each one scores at Serafim's Ephedrine Heaven and
drops off the planet, another click on God's
calculator — if only you could give it back
to the street, the way the street deals it out —
and then, with hardly a flicker, you're aboard
the Lavender Bay Ferry glimpsing Paradise,
1963: the Beatles rehearsing 'Twist & Shout',
a Luna Park sunset in faded Ektachrome
unspooling on a screen at the back of your mind,
the moving finger spelling out a lucky
number, the suburbs as close as a giant
face against yours, breathing, while utterly
elsewhere she's waiting in the Persian Room
tapping her nails on the laminex. Once
you were growing up through sunburns
summer by summer, in those leafy backstreets
full of parked cars. Then — it happened invisibly —
you were loafing on the dusty edge of Australia
or soaking in a tub, becoming fashionable
reluctantly, like the cigarette papers Dad used
that now endorse a more nitric habit.
The steam fogs the glass, and Abdul wipes it
with a cloth that's filthy, but it clears the view:
she's there, frowning, as the magazines taught her,
against a background of drifting pedestrians.

HAVING COMPLETED MY FORTIETH YEAR

Although art is, in the end, anonymous,
turning into history once it's left the body,
surely some gadget in the poet's head
    forces us to suffer

as we stumble through the psychology of it:
the accent betraying a class conflict
seen upside-down through a prism, the bad luck
    to be born in a lucky country —

yet in the end it is our fault, i.e. my fault
not to be born Frank O'Hara and cursing
a whole culture for it — it's no excuse
    not to be run over at thirty,

to live on, turning out couplets
with the fecundity of a sausage machine
but without the cachet of the Imperial drawl,
    not even a cute lisp;

above all to miss out on drugs and Sodom
in the mindless mid-afternoon heat among
the nylon swimsuits and the beery surfers,
    a trial, not a vacation —

the girl around the corner gagging on whisky
in the school-yard after dark, the boss
clocking off and weaving out the back door:
    'I'll be at the pub . . .'

well, at forty, the pieces lie about
waiting to be picked up and puzzled over
and fitted into a pattern, after a fashion,
    one I'm not fond of —

there are two sorts of people: those who say
with an owlish look 'There are two sorts of people',
and those who don't; then there are the writers
    who live on another planet,

their droppings bronzed like babies' booties
and we're glad to see things so transmogrified
though we suspect that life's not always rhymed
    quite as neatly as that,

and then there are those for whom every voyage
is an opportunity to lash the rowers,
the sun rising over something absolutely
    dreadful every day:

a people totally given to the cannibal virtues,
a set of laws designed to confuse and punish,
an art that shrinks experience into a box then
    hermetically seals the lid;

but squabbling over Modernism won't help,
England needs liberating but not by me,
she has concocted her own medications after all
    for marsh fever and the sinks,

so I'm stocking the fridge with Sydney Bitter,
checking the phone numbers of a few close friends
while the conservatives see to it that I conserve
    my sad and pallid art

and I'm hoping that the disk drive holds out
at least till the fag-end of the party
so my drunken guests may go on bopping till they
    drop into their mottoes

as I did some twenty years ago,
embarking on this yacht, this drudger's barge,
being 'absolutely modern' as my mentor taught
    from the embers of his youth,

and hardly guessing then what would turn up:
these postcard views from a twinkling and distant
colony, of the twin cities: dying heart of Empire,
    sunset on the Empire State.

LUFTHANSA

Flying up a valley in the Alps where the rock
rushes past like a broken diorama
I'm struck by an acute feeling of precision —
the way the wing-tips flex, just a little
as the German crew adjust the tilt of the sky and
bank us all into a minor course correction
while the turbo-props gulp at the mist
with their old-fashioned thirsty thunder — or
you notice how the hostess, perfecting a smile
as she offers you a dozen drinks, enacts what is
almost a craft: Technical Drawing, for example,
a subject where desire and function, in the hands
of a Durer, can force a thousand fine ink lines
to bite into the doubts of an epoch, spelling
Humanism. Those ice reefs repeat the motto
whispered by the snow-drifts on the north side
of the woods and model villages: the sun
has a favourite leaning, and the Nordic flaw
is a glow alcohol can fan into a flame.
And what is this truth that holds the grey
shaking metal whole while we believe in it?
The radar keeps its sweeping intermittent promises
speaking metaphysics on the phosphor screen;
our faith is sad and practical, and leads back
to our bodies, to the smile behind the drink
trolley and her white knuckles as the plane drops
a hundred feet. The sun slanting through a porthole
blitzes the ice-blocks in my glass of lemonade
and splinters light across the cabin ceiling.
No, two drinks — one for me, one for Katharina
sleeping somewhere — suddenly the Captain
lifts us up and over the final wall
explaining roads, a town, a distant lake
as a dictionary of shelter — sleeping elsewhere
under a night sky growing bright with stars.

SHADOW DETAIL

You press the bakelite button, and wait,
and wait. Presently the lift rattles
down to the ground floor, and the attendant
passes you something through the brass grille.

The chlorine sifts down through the water,
turning pastel blue. That woman floating
fifteen feet above the floor of the pool —
she's taking medication for weight loss,
a cheapskate pharmaceutical that stretches
and compresses the day until it disappears
into the hot white dot in the centre
of the screen. The thin man in the
viewfinder acts like an instructor —
'This is the patented exposure guide;
snap it open and look at the sunlight.'
Overhead a bumpy plane — a two-tablet bomber,
the man calls it, shading his eyes from the late
afternoon glare — laboriously scrawls a message
on the haze that tints the sky pink.

At last it's evening, and a chill breeze touches
the lawn. Now they're all staring at something
resting on the bottom of the pool. At least,
that's the way you read this photograph.
The shadow detail builds up, telling us
about their hair, the boy's dark tweed jacket,
pointing out details, the texture in the
broad masses. And the ancient lift creaks up
to its cage at the top of the building,
a cage the wind visits and teases.

PARALLEL LINES

1

parallel lines
autonomy, then breakfast

as if the coastal light were perfect
perfect in its tonal range and balance

let's have a slide show (Kodachrome)
and impress the (American) neighbours

meet Kathy, burst into tears,
a list of things to see and do

things I hope will make me happy
happy, not miserable

post blotto triste old chap
all animals are perfect

2

intersecting lines
astrology, then breakfast

the weather's just right for the
multi-coloured debris of bodies

imperfect notes, the Latin scribble
bottled deities

I trust them to make me powerful
at least, less anguished

3

we meet at last, old friend
I think you're enlightened:

the world climate has arranged itself,
do you realise that?

its power is really its needs, not
unconscious needs, but not conscious

good at night, bad in the morning
I wish to live to a great age

4

I think you're stoned again
or is that true love?

my need, my lack, is powerful
a malignant spirit, bad adaptation

but subtle and wonderful drugs . . .
Bayer, Merrell, Roche, et cetera

I'm grateful for those children, but
why do they get lost and angry?

dig deep and be generous
for your own sake, said the book

5

that horror's maladaptive
'suffering demeans': Maugham

failure of light at the end of the day
racing to finish the art-work

as the sedative descends
onto the vast subtly-coloured beach

live by the water, the fellow said
it's nice to be smart, but not enough

this pretty hologram you won't need
at the end of the road.

THOSE GODS MADE PERMANENT

Those gods made permanent by photochemistry
rise dripping from the tank of inky fluids,
rehearsing their tricks of significance —
one eyebrow lifted, a belly-laugh
practised to perfection, a smile
that writhes into a smirk then vanishes,
whole personalities built by the pharmacopoeia.
Voyaging from where they hatch in a late-night
session around the old Remington, cigar smoke
drifting through the venetian blinds, from
the fitful confabulations forming and re-forming
they spill into the glare, flapping erratically
across the huge darkened hangars, across
our foreheads, the friar and the harlot,
the makeshift Indian and his angry brother
pleading for revenge.
                                A lawbreaker beckons
and suddenly we're sucked down a secret tunnel
into the belly of the Weimar Republic, forced to
watch a detective hungry for victory hunt
and haunt his double through caves and labyrinths
that burrow under Berlin. The police are utterly
corrupt — or are they? Why am I frightened for
that criminal as he weaves his desperate escape,
turning at last into his best impersonation?

And when they whisper to us, we're lost
as soon as we listen, looking through a keyhole
as the Minister's daughter calls out something
innocent, but we know better — the scenery speaks
carelessly of a microphone under the bed
and a lamp blown out leaving us in darkness,
though not for long — soon the answers appear
one by one, blending in an intricate pattern
like a blanket of phosphorescent plankton rising

up to the moonlight breaking in flakes on the
surface of the sea.
                    And when that servant climbs
to polish his peculiar mirror we rise with him
up to where his small corner of the room
is swollen and the curved glass bloats his perch
into a throne. Down below, his breeding
shrunk to a gesture of appeasement, we spy
his master waiting with an anxious smile.
And now we see the slow sneer slide across
the devil's lips; we watch his eyes clouding
with a mist of sin and power as he reaches up
to buff the silvered globe, plausibly imitating
the pose of an Old Italian Master, as a chill dusk
falls on North London.
                    The red buses rattling
and belching black smoke as they trundle
around the corner circulate like money,
returning every night to the same depot,
and our trade with these spirits too has a
cash economy dimension, a give-and-take.
You pay for your ticket, and remember a friend
cranking out a crude impersonation — a laugh
practised at a party, a way of holding a girl's
elbow as she climbs out of a pickup truck,
and now he's folding his arms across his chest
and cocking his head on one side
like Woody Woodpecker — 'quizzical', that's
the word his raised eyebrow spells out.
He's saying that the tricks they teach us
are fragments of a style, and we can only
juggle them clumsily like a teenager
burning his fingers on a cigarette.

I believed everything they said. At first
their strategies were deft and generous,

they sketched an outline of a character
as likeable and yet as forceful as my own,
investing him with property, a kindly father
and a sister with a quick temper. They
laid out the plan of their adventure with care
and emotional economy, but a quarrel begins
and the close-up lenses get to work — one
wide-angle shot follows another, a scowl
leads quickly to a shout and a slap, a hand —
whose? — whips out a heavy black gun and fires —
and we find the plot folding up like a robot
and stumbling off in the wrong direction
too abruptly for us to get our bearings.
Is this all the reward we are offered
for our painstaking attention, for the strain
of our emotional investment? What we asked for
led to nothing, what we didn't want to see
        was made plain.

Your friend laughs, and says humorously
in the fluent quoted speech you both enjoy:
I'd often take a girl to the romantic epics
and watch the magic soak into her subconscious,
forcing a re-enactment of those passions
some time afterwards, delayed, then in haste,
to my great advantage. The costume dramas
provoked a disarray of costume and bare flesh,
the umlauts of the Alien Commander conjugated
to murmurings as familiar as underwear. But
things are reduced and the great palaces
shrunk to the corner of a sitting-room, now
art gets interrupted by a news flash — we're
inside an aircraft with a parachute platoon,
and the howling engines drown out everything —
here's a journalist scribbling awkwardly,

braced against a bulkhead, while the leader
points to gridiron diagrams on a blackboard —
then the floor of the plane drops away
and a rush of cold night air — no, it's bombs
that are tumbling down like grey logs
onto the tiny countryside, boiling into flame,
a rolling sheet of oily smoke — your money
paid for this, and for the historical figures
to suffer under a crushing load of politics,
each death perfectly adapted to its epoch.

And so the scenes unravel as they
must do, some long, some so brief
a glimpse encompasses them, and the story
constructs itself by stacking up
one incident against another,
the agile puppets clashing together
and interacting with these two-dimensional
representations of a bank, a bottle shop,
a clock, a loaded gun, and out of this
tangle of particulars rendered by a camera
the optic nerves fake a kind of motion —
and you supply an ending and a moral scaffolding
that locks the plot together in your brain.
But that's the mad professor's method
of looking at things — the obsessive neatness
gives it away. Could the whole industry, perhaps,
just be devoted to a blend of profit and escapism,
like the great frescos of the late Renaissance?
A man can stroll into a cinema, can't he,
to huddle out of the winter wind, just to
rest up for a while? If his future
glares back at him out of the screen
isn't he justifiably upset at how
his private miseries are spelt out?

Is the alcoholic — look, some of the viewers
are sobbing quietly — does he need to be
painted with such cruel precision? How often
have you given a start in the shadows,
watching shameful events unravel in front of
your neighbours, in brilliant colour, that
you thought were buried long ago? When you
stumble on the fact that the second-in-command
likes a drink, and has an old dog called Spot
that he's much too fond of, you know he'll
weaken at a crucial point — as the submarine's
about to dive, or just as the enemy troops come
clattering around the corner, their torches
        flooding the cobblestones —
doesn't your breath suck at the stuffy air,
your pulse falter, knowing full well
what you have done? The wretch stares up at you,
the torchlight glistening on his forehead,
and behind his eyes a struggle is illuminated,
        a man against a demon.

Your friend slinking out of a porno movie —
we know what sort of kisses are his
special favourites, we've seen them
smeared across a screen, mouthing
'Give me, give me!' like a greedy child.
I've seen the track of money, how it trickles
from the box office to someone's bank account,
how it pays for prostitutes and crank drugs;
how when you pay to enter, your money
bullies and threatens the poor,
it buys bestiality and any horror
your heart can invent. So he leaves, exhausted;
another crowd pushes in to be next at the feast.
And the family movie, like a giant sponge, with
emotions washing through it, back and forth.

Do they feel better after a good cry? Those
crybabies? weeping through the two-hankie talkies?
I want to be gentler, teasing the audience
so they chuckle, not sob; at the end of the show
death knocks us down, I've seen it happen,
and then you're really alone.
Perhaps I wanted too much from the future,
the same generosity that washed over the rows
of seats, a thousand coloured possibilities.
This loss well up and floods the present,
blurring its dull practical gadgets, the past
making a tear-duct attack — there should be
a flush system to blow out the memory banks
so I could ready myself for these apparitions:
the buses puttering through the English twilight,
those German police drinking champagne, the master
waiting in attendance at the foot of the servant's
ladder, smiling miserably, a gang of friends
laughing still in that playground long ago —
so much is changed utterly, the pale
beam spells out in its flickering.

I asked a girl out too, and bought her popcorn
and explored the mystery of manners in the gloom,
those complicated secrets, but all that has aged
and decayed, the woman who was once the type
of perfection and a warm scented angel
has succumbed to the human in her destiny
as I must, also, one day. The years
punish those of us who survive them
is one way to look at it, and if the sight
of a torn movie poster flapping in the wind
upsets you, so it should, the slope is
downhill now and the strange valley ahead
is brimming with darkness, where your father's ghost
waits to welcome you into the company of shadows.

DURING THE WAR

During the War I was sent to Wilson,
south of Sydney. It's pretty country:
long low hills, cut by jagged gullies.
The people thereabouts
are farmers and shopkeepers mostly,
and like to keep to themselves.

One night I heard a whisper in the pub,
confidential information from a criminal
that a large-scale trade in crooked liquor
was being set up. A bad piece of work.
A Doctor Davis, Donald Night (alias
'Donald the Dog'), a publican named Waterbird,
and others, they were buying black,
mainly from Military Canteens in the country.
They paid Waterbird to pick up the liquor,
and he boasted he'd carted truckloads of it
to a certain garage at Blackacre.

I need a shot of coffee, to jog the memory,
or one of those truth drugs — my Notebook —
all this was so long ago, distant
rain on the foothills, drawing closer,
the gullies running with muddy water.

Sometimes I passed on valuable tips
to stray criminals, partly tit for tat,
to repay my dues, partly for my name —
you have to be known as a straight man
or you're as good as dead.

The detectives that I talked to told me
that bad things happened in the 1940s,
you had to keep your eyes open and your trap
shut; and a gun handy, if you had one.

There were times when I felt bound,
struggling to do right.

My Notes: criminals like Hartfeld
seem to be in touch with how the cat jumps
in the city. Confidentially I will tell you:

All political parties have what is called
a bag-man, they gather up funds
for hidden tricks and for fighting
a battle or two. Each week the operators
are called up from their heavy and confused
sleep; they're doing the right thing,
in their dreams, and they offer heaps.

One fine day I got a ring from a contact:
he whispered that his new friends were
skipping town early in the morning.
The weather was clear, cool and bright,
but I could see a ridge of cloud gathering
behind the hills. 'Now every dog's in trouble,'
Donald said, 'and I want help, but the Boss
lost his cutting edge long ago, and
the Party Fund with it. The crims,
they loaded some furniture in the back
of the van, and stacked the liquor
in the front,' Donald said, 'that's
how they got it here. That truck
had travelled over a thousand miles.'

I said 'If you are here tonight
I will dump you, as I promised.'
He replied 'You're a tough Bastard.
I just drove the truck. I done nothing wrong.
I can give you a lot of "Tip-offs",
I can help you in many ways. Can I

see you face-to-face and talk it over?'
I said 'The die is cast, old son.'
I rang off. How many so-called friends
had he sold down the river?

'What is the setup?' I asked. 'You are a
country man,' the Boss replied,
'and the Local Member doesn't know you.
He gives the bag to the Commissioner
and the buck stops there.
Whichever party gets the votes
controls the Company.' They have
both hands out, day and night,
to get money by hook or by crook.

My Green Notebook, in faded blue ink:
Kitty was killed for taking customers
from Diamond Doyle's Brothel, my contact said.
She had been terribly bashed and mutilated.
Later a journalist named Larry Latch
from the *Melbourne Truth* made me a lucrative
offer behind the pub, no one looking,
and I showed him affidavits I'd obtained
from various people, some very respectable.
But I couldn't give him the particulars
officially, and I couldn't let him print them —
I would be sacked for Breach of Discipline.
I contacted the Commissioner and his
lap dogs — they seemed suspicious and afraid.

To the Editor: 'I will clean this mess up
quick smart. Call a General Inquiry
and let any crook tell us all he knows.'

The Commissioner is back from his holidays —
he was accompanied by two prostitutes,

one of whom was wanted on Warrant. He and I
had a heated debate, and I heard later
he was shot at in the street by the criminal
Hartfeld, who had also wounded a bystander
in Wilkinson's gun shop in Queen Street
when he had stolen firearms and ammunition.

I rang a Senior Officer (name deleted)
at the Company and gave him the nod.
Joe Pyramus rang me the following day
and said he had booked me a Sleeping Berth
on the Southern Flyer that night to Sydney
and I had to meet him, like it or not.
I told him the Brothels were connected
with the blackmarket liquor. He asked how.
Kitty was found murdered in her kitchen;
Hartfeld's blood-stained clothes were burnt
under the fuel heater in the basement there.
His girl-friend gave me this information and
I swear it was true. I gave it to Joe.
But I couldn't tell anyone who gave me
the good oil, not even my oldest friends.

Then I heard that Hartfeld had left Sydney
that day in the company of the Commissioner.
The next night I saw his car, a 1940 Buick,
in the main street. There were two men
in the car, and I photographed them.
Here are some of the decent ones I took.
I searched the car and found a large
quantity of cigarettes in the boot
and two new military tyres. That was it.
I drew my service pistol and said
'Put up your hands and turn around.
I'm going to search you.' One had no fingers
on his left hand, and a broken jaw.

Hartfeld said 'It's a fair cop. I'm unlucky.
You nabbed me at Paradise. When I got out
I went home. I met The Don, an old friend,
and he asked me to come up to the country.
I suppose I'm a dead man now.'
I told him 'If you go back to Sydney
you will be done in.' He said
'I don't give a damn for that; I know
the graft and dishonesty that is going on,
who's who, and who does their dirty work.
But I'm safe down there. I give orders,
I don't take them.' He went back to Sydney
and was shot dead two nights later.

(Telephone call from Sydney — I'm staying
incognito in Mrs Anderson's Hotel.
The message: 'A gang of criminals
is flogging crook liquor from hotels at Lithgow,
Wilson, and the Oxford Military Camp Canteen.
It is stored in a garage in Blackacre owned by
the Premier of New South Wales.')

Note: I was absent on leave during 1944.
The day I returned, I met the Boss
on the front veranda. It had been raining
the night before, and the muddy street
was a mass of tangled footprints.
Two couples were walking in the direction
of Anderson's Hotel. They waved to the Boss
and he said 'Those are theatrical people.
They've just come back from Brisbane,
where they entertained the Diggers.
They've come here for a spell to rest.'
I pounced. 'You're wrong! That mongrel
in the grey fur coat is Donald Night, alias
"Donald the Dog". He is a very bad criminal.

The tall girl is Diamond Doyle, who runs
a brothel at Kings Cross.' He laughed at me.
He said: 'You're a pup, and you know nothing.'

Thunder, rolling over the wet grass,
and a flicker of lightning. Note: Talk to
an officer I know in Southern Queensland.

Deposition: 'I refused to go on Transfer,
I said the Company could sack me
and I would pick up the threads from there.'

The driver signalled me over. He said,
pointing to the rear seat, 'This is
the man you want, the Top Boss.'
He said 'Get in.' I asked him his name
and he gave me some fictitious moniker.
I recognised him right off. I said 'Your name
is Joe Blake, also known as George Black.
I arrested you nine years ago at Paradise with
Doctor Davis, then using the name of Hartfeld.'
He said 'Your Transfer has been cancelled.'

The sky was filled with cloud, and heavy mist
covered the paddocks. I admit I was worried.
There was a sharp cracking sound, and a flash
of light. The truck had crashed
through the railing and down into the gully,
and they were all dead when we reached them.

The kid ran up to me and yelled
'Quick! The new guard has been shot!'
He was still clinging to the gun
that Hartfeld had shot him with. He said
'He got me through the back. I had a go —
I didn't squib it.' These were his last words.

The Commissioner told me I was due for the drop.
'Don't bother about the Brothels now,' he said.
'You never should have left the country,
where you had lots of decent friends
and reliable informers, to come to this
terrible place. You are alone now,
and always will be. You cannot make a move.
This is a Breach of Discipline. Be still.'

SEX CHEMISTRY

a sequence

1. *Childhood*
2. *Boarding School*
3. *Papyrus*
4. *After The Dance*
5. *Party Line, 1956*
6. *Haberdashery*
7. *Poolside*
8. *Spin-the-Bottle*
9. *Three Hand-coloured Photographs*
10. *Crosstalk*
11. *At The Newcastle*
12. *The Little Engine*
13. *Sonnet: Country Music*
14. *Affairs of the Heart*
15. *Delirium*
16. *Sonnet: Lullaby*
17. *Trolley*
18. *Life Class*
19. *Dirty Weekend*
20. *Khaki*
21. *Modern Art*
22. *Malaya, 1926*
23. *La Pulqueria*
24. *Hack Writer*

1. CHILDHOOD

Beautiful memories,
that seaside holiday,
tossing and not sleeping,
dreaming but not dreaming,

she begs you rather than
sleep to shop properly,
to stop kidding. Sweetheart,
I'd say as much for you,

you in your loopy gloom
high in the bell tower,
thinking and dreaming
like a sponge, silly boy.

Until you do it,
you have no right —
before that we wore badges,
tin hearts that glowed,

signs of a boy growing
into a beautiful
young woman — deciphered
it, did you? Clever bitch!

Boarding school daydreams . . .
oh how I wanted to
wake up a hot-headed
drama queen — damn you all!

Bright gods, trust me to play
the game properly. Meeting you
suddenly, I think you're tops;
I'm absolutely riddled by lust

at least I think it's lust.
In the morning the room is cold.
I mutter under the silver rose, alone,
gaping at the disappearing universe.

Breakfast matters: you're there.
Is it love? Look out, bossy-boots,
some among us have been thus bedevilled.
Bothered thus, I natter, happily.

At the coming-around of the clockwork
and the gathering-in of the rosters
the chatterers remember everything;
the whole dining room is lucid.

The daylight passes in a daze of weather.
We're imperfect, but that's perfect.
In the dark we'll be truly happy,
as animals are, my precious.

I'm tall and clever, but is that
enough? I'm only an amateur, and
I don't want the pillow talk.
Turn on the darkness. Impress me.

3. PAPYRUS

Look at Egypt, sunning itself. We
took the camera; now sit on the stool.
The pistol is full of blanks.
Don't speak French, whatever you do!

Rome, O Painted Whore, you are a sight
for sore eyes, or for our attempts
at abstract art, the billy on the boil,
prison gas leaking outside

the walls. Is it rat poison? I'm
wearing red silk for my passions,
the priest said. It cultivates them.
Kids kiss innocently, like cocoa butter.

I'm spelling dirty words out
for the girls. It's easy. Like
'he was tossed on the wave
passion drowned him under.'

Darling, I am restless for your
. . . skin burning . . .
. . . touch!' A grass fire
and . . . fever . . .

(married women) . . . hetaerae,
their kisses
and . . . (cried out) . . .
were . . . (broken) . . .

4. AFTER THE DANCE

Someone has raked the driveway smooth,
someone has turned the porch lamp on, how
thoughtful. Small town nightfall: young folk
gather for the old-time dance, the ligatures,
    the bonding rituals.

Comb your hair, sweetheart, your Prince
has come. On the gravelled river-bed
weeds are plaited together the way
we are entangled, pussy-foot, in a
    dance of destiny.

The picture of a wheel spinning makes you dizzy
as the frame emotions skid out of sight. She
thinks she's making me happy, ha, have a drink.
Where they flash the two-coloured dog
    the speeding stylus writes.

I see the Roman pens moving in the gloom,
they flex, they make me powerful, malign
stars glitter and rain down, they won't stop
The storm learning . . . bodies, tangled
    . . . struggle for love

curtains lazy close beach flood
broken bridge at the end of the track. I watch
. . . river swollen . . . can't help what this
Towards the future this pretty . . . marriage
    small town . . . catastrophe . . .

5. PARTY LINE, 1956

A tryst, heavy breathing in the back seat,
on the secret road behind the mountain,
raining, glimpsed through glass, pink
underwear tangled on the floor — listen, kids,
Mum's new freedom chatters down the wires,
on a circuit board the whole town
links into, wow, hot gossip,
the sexiest mum in the valley.

Saturday afternoon the farmers
watch the main street close down
at closing time. Things are getting
more modern every day, aren't they?

In black-and-white, on an old Admiral TV,
under the splintered ice an enemy submarine
strikes at the roots of capitalism.
She does her exercises on the carpet
in a brief halter top, a neighbor watching
through the half-closed venetians. Here,
the sunlamp tans her in twenty minutes,
the real thing in a day and a half.

Glow and glitter, Karen — kiss the
trumpeter if you can stand his lip,
the Jazz Waltz is about to start.
Start too soon — look: this brings
hot clutching and flashed angry looks,
disaster and discovery during the samba.

And broken coffee-cups at breakfast time.
The kitchen door slams. Then the screen
door bangs shut after her, apron flapping,
sobbing down the garden path.

Hey, you there with the scented lipstick,
take me to the bosses and their club, if
they exist, these functionaries. I love to
flirt with money, and the idea of large money
writhing in a bundle under the weight of politics.
Cleverly spoken, Debbie, you're a top girl —
are you on the loose? Hmmm, looks good. But . . .
catching you, I'm catching someone else's germs.

Our hostess and accumulator of lies,
presiding at the barbecue, her looks astray,
catches two wives in a warm embrace,
how can they help it, their husbands utterly
rattled in the face of their girlish needs,
they're so bright and I'm retreating into headache.
I'm all knocked up, this moody weather. Shame,
mechanical in its operation, a real shame.

From each emotion manager, wrote
one of the husbands in a last attempt,
frowning and clutching his head, to each
worker in the factories of passion . . .
but the salesman of love had lost his touch,
and in the foaming pool each foray discovered
another girl wearing a blank look of bliss.

The hostess watches me. Am I her only male?
Snappy dresser! while others to a feast depart
hence from regiments of the unhappy —
while the busy host was getting drunk.
Then he and the girl tried on the same size
dresses and the chatter dispersed, two or more
of the shop assistants crazy about her.

7. POOLSIDE

The host climbs out, soaked and spitting oaths,
and a teenage girl leaves the barbecue.
Two of those drinks your wife mixed,
bright pink and cheerful, and I'm
seeing double: breasts, twin headaches
exactly the same size await me
frowning from each temple, and a diptych
concusses the chatter: a car salesman
hitting his better half. A pygmy politics emerges
wherever two or more of you are gathered,
shopping together. All right, stop biting,
I'd much rather sleep with you than with
that other poltergeist. You're greedy,
aren't you? O Painted Laugh, why is your
belly convulsing? Can 'a man' become a sign
for 'a muscular spasm'? Horoscope,
betray yourself, take me back to a feast,
if this is a feast, these glib flirtations,
the whole gang badly knocked out
by the mundane speech the flame attempts,
each sleep a cancelled cheque, as I
watch myself thinking of you, deracinated
Sweetheart, boarding a Greyhound.

8. SPIN-THE-BOTTLE

While you stare at the sex magazines,
the pink flesh racked on the newsstand,
in your back pocket an origami emotion
unfolds itself, lucky to be breathing
close to your real need, your grocery
shopping, while an old rat with nothing to say
says it bravely and says it well.
Oh, the spill on the kitchen floor,
the drink spinning, and the bottle!
Is this adolescent kissing and hot fondling
merely an entertainment? Is it more,
a 'learning curve', perhaps? Learning,
c'est la vie, O Lucky Duck!
Those mottoes you embroidered on my heart
still burn, burn more deeply with each
passing year — leafy doubter,
green critic, take your smile away,
let the sky go black and shitty if it must.
Who dares, wins, playing strip poker
in the motel room with a loose blonde
and a bottle of Jim Beam. Then — it happened
too quickly for Brett to get his heart out —
the girls were in love, in an age when that was
futile, 'Before Sexism', I mean, 'Before Feminism'.
Flirting with the Westerners was a duty,
and fashionable, so we all did it. Lighting
cigarettes, is there a trick in that?
The light here is awful, Mister President.
But the view of magazines and drifters appeared
as a print, whose surface was only a surface,
neighbour to lust if looked at hard enough.

9. THREE HAND-COLOURED PHOTOGRAPHS

One

He grew like her, then more like her,
in the summer sun oiled and baking. Was that
towel hers? — now it was his. Look, he's asleep,
reddening. The parked cars, their surfboards
dozing in the heat.

Two

It's no fun for the old folk,
becalmed in the sexual tropics; lobotomised
by the menopause. A dose of the eye-drops, then
a flash on the screen as the Doris Day
movie disappears.

Three

She wakes up certain someone
loves her. Then by lunch-time she's in a flood
of tears. She waters the cactus in the caravan park.
If only her love-life were under control . . .
Student nurses!

The way you lie there, it's an opinion, those
bronze medal limbs, the sheets crumpled,
your body the site and centre of conspicuous
waste. It's a vote against the mob,
the way you flick the lamp out, thoughts
akimbo, and stare at the visual display.
Sleep, says the computer.

It sounds brilliant in the dark, at 2 a.m., that
breathing in stereo, so crisp, or rain
in the mesh grille of a microphone.
Is it recording a storm, or sound effects?
The machine listens to its own astrology. Who
left the screen on? That red, that luminescent
green, I must be sleepwalking. Toast,

ham and eggs for two, all on the video.
Does a wish flicker, like that?
Then you disappear leaving a faint ghost
and go to black, as the program dumps
a bracelet of digits in the outboard memory.
The printout spelling doom, do you carry it
with you through sleep, a gift, a poison?

And when you wake at sunrise, heavy breather,
golden in the light, will you be content?
Hush — the shower's whispering, breakfast is ready,
and two expensive German microphones wait for
breath, for movement, for the trace of your desire.

The last sunlight filters into the bar
      through the bottle glass:
a green drink in a green shade . . . that's
how the country's run. Great Calculator,
      make light of this burden.

My little number, bless her soul, she's
      safe at home in the suburbs.
Unravelling her cares, the pink rinse
Den Mother ravishes the Armchair Bolshevik,
      and the spent executive.

Your spouse, Smiler, was in here a while ago,
      looking pretty crook,
her nerves shot to pieces, reminiscing: a young
girl, old times, rock on the idiot box
      making your nerves jump.

Well, they were the days, of course.
      Time flies, old son.
Another one for you, Kevin? Well . . .
One more gin and tonic for the lady.
      Time, gentlemen, please.

12. THE LITTLE ENGINE

Tears drenching the windscreen, the little Ford
determined to see and do everything, pathetic
fallacy, that is, those two metonymically
    in the little car

burst through a travel list, not miserable at all,
see, you bullshit artist! Even changing gears
you make me happy, chopping through the astrology
    that bottles me up.

O Coloured One, crisp as cellophane, telephone
the modems of the West Coast, if they can be
contacted on the Bell Protocol, and tell them,
    ludic devices,

how perfect I am in my corruptible body, how
luminous when held in your gaze, and how this
clutch of signs betrays us to the bosses,
    despite our intentions —

it's true, born out of burning bodies there are
malignant spirits, but also benevolent ones
fevering to save this ratshit imperium,
    everyone in it;

in the glow given off by smouldering paper
the little engine struggles to be real. That light
fails, but I meet you in the morning in the car park,
    demented and alive.

13. SONNET: COUNTRY MUSIC

A friend said to me the other day
for goodness' sake, what's the harm,
a real live woman. It's a crying shame.
As for her, she's crazy about you. She did
bundle up her memories, tossed them aside,
astray. Sleeping, she begs you to stay.
Part of this is bad faith, part mere male
snares tangling with a woman's wiles.

A while back, emerging from marriage, you were sad.
Sad, and about as safe as a loaded gun.
Skin like peaches and cream. It's fate.
Pin my heart to your sleeve, just for fun.
Snap me up, I'm lonesome. Ain't that a shame,
a guy like you, take it, all my loving.

Affairs of the heart, they say.
Fortunate, those who can care.
Print the body count, the harm alarms.
A spare personality begins to spin

out of control. Their bodies, then their minds
aspire to more before darkness, can
damage more domestic love than all
animal hatred may. This doesn't happen.

Is this madness what it's about? This
slipping, breakage, she hopes repair can't
be long away. Kissing brings ease.
Beware, they dream, the thirst of lips.

Spin faster, delirious stars.
Pining won't help, so let's begin
snooping about, caring a little, loving
again, all those ridiculous things.

15. D E L I R I U M

Lightning strikes twice: For whose sake
is all this disrobing? *Mal de mer*, 'suffering
devils for love.' I need a sedative, honey-bun,
    herbal or carnivore.

Please me how you will, if you will, please.
You're sweet, but stupidly blind to the vast
and powerful blotto crank motives tricking both
    our bodies on a bed.

Don't ask me why I dwell here, in a rundown
motel, drinking badly, dozing off in a deck chair,
only waiting for your special conspiratorial knock
    to slowly grow young.

Beautiful powders, speak to me! You cure arthritis,
you make women into ravishing girls again, ask me
why I dawdle here in the backyard of a career,
    soaking up sunlight,

among the talking books, the blind and the lame,
adapting heaven and earth to my dirty purposes.
Great writers speak to the world of men from
    the Southern Hemisphere,

marvelling at the damage they cause, the kindness
the best of them are capable of, waiters of our thirst.
Delirium. Outside someone opens a keg. Tears gather
    beside your dreaming body.

16. SONNET: LULLABY

I'm not jealous of your pet executives —
their coma therapy, their new guitars.
The latest boy-friend's hardly seventeen,
isn't that what the tabloids say?
In the cheap hotel, the heaps of magazines —
You Can't go Back to Woop Woop, sobs
the big print. And the speed jerking
up the spinal column to its spasm above.

Now the sea heaps itself on the pillow
with its wacky promises, and you're floating
through the ceiling again. Tell sex to go
back to the playpen where it came from. Your
future's waiting: suburbia loud with radios,
telling you to wake up now, and do the shopping.

17. TROLLEY

In the trolley, her foamy underwear.
You see wandering bright spots, don't you?
Your stomach falls out. You're not
     what you used to be.

Crush the minted ice and fill the glass,
in italic, please. The splinters make it real,
the fragments of light in the flashing liquid.
     Drink one for me.

Back to the trolley — she has to sleep somewhere,
why not here, in the wreckage? You like
the wrecked career, and the way it glitters?
     Take one: it's free.

Explain the mask, explain the water-bed,
and the sudden feeling of mob rule fed by
glossy magazines and French cookery books.
     Look; you can see

the vast purple firmament fretted with gold,
the snowfields like writing paper in the moonlight
tied up with flex and piano wire to keep you
     anxiety-free.

Now we do 'The Smile', keeping time to the music.
Now she gulps madly at the glass decanter. Smash
that on the patio, a guest advises, do 'The Slipperoo'.
     Why not, busy bee?

Back to the trolley, and how to conclude it.
She could strip naked, I guess that's the answer,
in the method known as 'Ducking for Apples'.
     Duck thus, and be free.

18. LIFE CLASS

Drink quickly, then enact just
what it's like to be very mad,
please, the madness of Life Drawing,
let's say, sketching naked bodies

day after day, enact that,
by hand, not by computer,
sober up and do it again,
this time be sensitive, truly,

not like the critics who pretend,
yes it was good for me, that book,
I loved it really, the lying shits.
Smoke some dope and then do it

more and more often, you'll like it,
being a lunatic just for a day,
or an hour, that's enough,
you'll get the flavour, the message:

now you know some of it, just like
the madness of loving, the flame
regarding itself in the mirror,
tow-truck colliding with tow-truck,

the logic of greed, the damage
and burning destruction. Drink up,
women await you, the sunlight
withdrawing silently to the West.

My husband doesn't know and wouldn't care
how smart you are, pretty boy. How did you adapt
your fuck-truck style of driving to a foreign car?
The way you dress, the deep looks, how painful.
A paint job, murmurs the sea, skin deep;
mid-life crisis, says the fashion magazine.
Is that shack a motel? Really? And
the local champagne, so ethnic . . . see how
the small town dies in the dead of winter.
They are embalmed, the grey, the soon-to-rise:
a shopping spree waits behind a wall of money
for its casualties, and you, blond sparkler,
with your sunlamp tan and sleight of hand
are a token passed between women. A breeze
speaking of summer, tinted Serepax Pink,
blows in through the screen door
and a naked couple rise groaning
out of their sweat — they're animal
dreams, in the mirror, aren't they?
floating into my holidays. Yes, I'd
like to be indelible, a perfect bruise.
Down here at the bottom of a whisky glass
you're staring at the bill, waiting
for your jackpot to fall out of my mouth;
you should know better, cheap trick, but then
you're new to the game, aren't you?
Here, clothe your idiot wishes in a
fifty-dollar kiss and let me sleep that
dreamless sleep that's more a kind of grieving,
then watch me haunt your future, blurred,
half erased, like a red tattoo.

20. K H A K I

Of one oddly fevered and
disguised as a deaf-mute
or a damaged attack jet

the fashionable lie details
her sex lost in his gaze
how it zaps you to death

the booze promises broken
purple heart, metal limbs,
ink touring your body

a medic tests a scalpel site
with a felt pen your fear
folds up like a penknife

in jail they keep you busy they
turn the light out, in the dark
life is faster so take the pill

and you can hear yourself talking
the grille covers something bad
recording a lie, a calculation

your fate is weighed up by
machine and no one listens
shaped like a strongman

the political left gets used to
the way the right used to live
and grows to like it, hard at my

gift I must keep jabbing at it
disappearing down the drain
gold and black, as princes were

The subject of the prank must not know
his own brother is speaking to him
through the tube. Do you think you can
do that? While I check the motor,
the turbo-charger, and the laundry pump.

It took so long to build these lies,
it's damn near impossible to give them up.
Each, a beautiful woman recollected
in tranquillity, their wavering bodies
reflected in the stream where they came
down to bathe, whispered the Narrator. Later,

when my favourite had done up her shoes,
we nibbled each other — those fumes —
is the Demon Alcohol climbing with us?

That child painter — why is his mouth gripping
the brush? Jesus! I'm shaking, make a wish,
quickly! She keeps biting her fingers.
Only great art can do this to us.

I'm speaking in metaphors, boys;
metaphors that are meant to make you cry.
Your faith is weak and anal, it will
get you nowhere. Tied to your mind is a body,
and it bangs head-on into your fate; you
are both your body, and its fatal desires.

22. MALAYA, 1926

How much more hot climate rainfall
can I stand, it feeds your unconscious
needs at night, I think you're
standing on my fate, my lack, a posh
    hut but subtle

and women's barter, silly child, for
mutton do they sell themselves, hard
done by and be gone to hogget, those
fine chattels, I mean womanish speakers,
    silent their heavy hearts.

I live by what I mean and do, this pretty
prefect and his tantrum notwithstanding.
After tennis, gin slings in the long
humid afternoons, nitric acid turning
    into tears, my dear.

Your devotion makes me happier than any pet,
though I think I make me happiest, dearest,
intersecting my doom with dippy wishes like a
perfect schoolgirl unaware of my 'growing
    womanly powers' Good Lord

it's real I must live forever, in this body,
the Latin spell forsakes us at the gates of death
and this truth dawning makes me powerful:
the right to grow and flourish in a climate of love;
    not to die of thirst.

23. LA PULQUERIA

The dance floor is the threshing floor. The next day
she gets up at dawn and carries a string bag
along the arroyo, looking for the spangled motto
that will win her father the holiday prize. Then
flame bursts from the shower instead of water.

He opens the safe — under the sacks of cash
are glass phials filled with pale blue tears;
evidence that the garbled speech of the poor
is rich with hidden meaning that only their priests
have the key to, and they're keeping mum.

The lovely widow is sweeping the courtyard;
an agile young man drenches her with promises
from the lime tree, then from the balcony.
He grins as she drinks the *pulque,*
and it spills over her blouse. She stumbles! —

She's skinned her tits, ape-face! Knockout
drops . . . the thick green glass tumbler
bounces across the linoleum when I faint and drop
everything. Now she wants to go rowing
on the lake, the water sprinkled with stars.

Thus God teaches us a necessary astronomy,
recharging our batteries for the Dance.
When I kiss you, the lovely young woman says,
the planets rotate like a tractor threshing
attachment — now will you marry me?

He reads a lot of Westerns and he
doesn't take holidays. He likes himself,
so he writes about the same kind of cove:
dodgy, tannic, erudite, the spine
with two staples that he really is.

On his working world cruise he sat on deck
and wrote about God, poker, coloured pigeons,
'my wife reading my ponderings', then
'my wife arguing' about the real purpose
of her dreams, and what their snapshots mean.

In their romantic historical novels they live out
their courtship, 'full of love for each other',
a dreadful warning to their children — what a mess
art can make of your bad habits. Art, sex,
gin, purple prose — the selfish baroque.

Then his 'Love Verses' appeared — poetry,
the arena where our sexual underworld emerges,
despite the linguists — and there he displayed
the mordant words and the cheap women
that made him invincible and proud.

He revealed too much to the critics!
So he sits in his deck chair, furious, writing
a story about a young hitchhiker, how she
takes the high road — 'I hear damaged drums
colliding head-on with the hit parade.'

In a letter to his biographer he admits
'This filth is what I love.' And later:
'Dark sparkles thrown off by the wine remain.'
Perhaps he means 'bright sparks thrown off
by the gin.' Ready to flash out of his mouth.

The program begins with a scene of a man, alone in a room, reading what is written on a piece of paper. The television glows in a corner. He is smoking. He looks out through a shaded balcony to a harbour. We see the harbour, the boats.

In another room, a room without a view, a woman is packing. Then she answers the telephone. Then we see a European city, from the air. The film appears grainy, the colours bleached. She waits at an airport departure lounge. We see the word 'Departures' in blue on a white background. The signs are in English.

He is leaning over the balcony rail, still smoking a cigarette. We see a telephone on a small white table beside him, an open book, and a tall glass half full of drink.

She is on board a plane. She looks out the window. We see cloud, layers of white cloud. We see her face in profile. It appears to have no expression. The make-up has been skilfully applied.

A long plume of smoke issues from his mouth. He wishes for certainty, but as his wish is a general one — he doesn't wish to be certain about any particular thing or emotion — as his wish is a general one, it will be denied by the transactions of his daily life.

He is absorbed by what is passing through his mind: letters, snatches of conversation, moving coloured images with no sound that must be fragments from a television document-ary. These things find themselves transfigured — dignified, perhaps — by the context of a love affair.

She may be going to leave. She is going to leave. She will leave. She will have left by now. She left. She has left.

Sitting in the aircraft she is surrounded by noise, and a vast relief. And a vast anxiety. What if she has done the wrong thing? What if she has done the right thing, but only on her own terms, the right thing *by herself* as it were? What if she has done the right thing by him, but damaged him all the same? Who will forgive her? She will be forgiven, she will have been forgiven, by time, by the passage of time, and that is enough. She would like a drink. She has a drink. She has had a drink.

He sits in a rented room, his father's son, staring at the television. What is he watching? He couldn't say. When he feels that life is too much for him he becomes agitated. He picks things up, fiddles with them, and puts them down again, misplacing them. His face goes pale and he knows he looks unwell. 'You don't look so good,' his friends remark. 'Is anything the matter?' He doesn't know how to answer them. He tries to relax, breathing deeply, but it only gets worse. The problem is, he thinks, he doesn't exercise enough. And yet he seems quite healthy. At least he seldom gets sick. Though he seldom looks one hundred per cent fit. He should exercise more.

He should go out more. When he left his wife and child — for reasons we won't go into here — he thought he'd be out all the time, having endless sexual adventures. But adventures are full of danger, aren't they? And now he's afraid.

She remembers the way her mother used to wait for the bus to the hospital, always knitting, surrounded by parcels — food, a flask of hot water, a magazine, the pink wool. Her eyes bewildered. Afraid of things about to go out of control. Her daughter waits for a flight call, but there are no flight calls any more. The baggage clerk told her that, but she didn't want to believe him. When she gets angry, her face flushes red and her fingers work themselves into fists, claws, fists, claws. Then she relaxes herself with a visible effort.

She is clean in her personal habits. She showers twice a day —
once in the morning, after her run; once after work, before
the night's adventures. She uses perfume sparingly, her hair is
clean, she exercises often, she believes that frequent sexual
adventure is the spice of life and good for the complexion.
She seldom reads books as she has quite enough reading to
get through at work, thank you, or so she says. She fears she
has cancer, and that her friends have cancer. She has believed
this for years, despite evidence to the contrary.

Sure, I'd like a drink. Just a beer. Thank you. Are you a nurse?
Oh, I don't know, I just thought . . . Yes, I like those prints.
Paintings, yes. They look great. No thanks, I think I'll just
have a coffee. Oh, all right. Yes, make it a strong one. No,
I'm fine. I love your hair, the way it smells. It smells good. I
left them. I don't want to go into the reasons. I worry about
the boy. He's only four. Growing up without a father. I'd
rather not talk about that. Can I see you Thursday? Friday,
then? We could go sailing, I have a friend with a boat. Well,
would you like to go to a nightclub? I didn't mean to get
angry. I'm sorry. I think I love you. Sure, I suppose that's a
bit heavy, but I can't help the way I feel. Sure. Okay, sure.
Why did you hang up when I rang before? Was it something
I said? I just like you, that's it, I mean I like you a lot.

According to the subtitles at the bottom of the screen, he is
trying to improve his state of mind. Rule number one. He
should stop believing that he must feel loved or accepted by
everybody for everything he does. He drinks too much, and
too often. Doesn't he? He smokes incessantly. No, he never
counts the cigarettes. He tries to be kind, to hold back the
quick sarcastic comment. He is a grown man, his music is
respected, such as it is. In the matter of close personal rela-
tions, he has made the break. He doesn't need his father's
forgiveness any more. Forgiveness for what? What failure,
what betrayal?

And that woman, now somewhere over the Pacific Ocean, he can find another one, can't he? There are plenty more where that one, that beautiful one, came from. Aren't there? He is a man, isn't he? He is free, isn't he? Free of what? He believes that he must feel loved or accepted by everybody for almost everything he does.

What's wrong with you? You look dreadful. Can I get you a drink? God it's dark in here, isn't it? You look lonely. Hey, would you like to come to my place and have sex? All right, don't faint, would you like to come to my place and make love?

I like you running your fingers down my back. You look worried, are you okay? You sure? Listen, I'm sleepy, I've got a hell of a day coming up at work. I always get up at this time. Sure, you can use the shower. I'll have one when I get back from my run. No, not Thursday, I'm going out. With this athlete, he's a long distance runner. Oh, I'll make the distance, don't you worry. Listen, sweetheart, I don't want you getting too wrapped up in this thing, okay? No, Friday's out. Maybe a nightclub or something Saturday night. No, I'll be in San Francisco next week. There's a big convention coming up. Why, are you interested in cosmetics? It's a real growth area. Oh, you're into music, I forgot. Rock music? Oh, I see. No, I don't get to concerts that often. Listen, sweetheart, I'm really busy at work. You could phone me at home, that would be better. Sure, any time between six and seven. Yes, I like you. San Francisco, maybe a month.

He is still trying to improve his state of mind, it appears from the evidence of the subtitles. But his actions — smoking, drinking, groaning on that exposed balcony — his actions indicate he is having difficulties, to say the least. Rule number two. He should give up the notion that he must act competently, adequately and achievingly. Well, he thinks, I will practise failure. I will fail at this and that, I will go on, nothing so terrible will happen, I'll learn to live with failure. Failing to hold down a decent job, failing to make a marriage work, failing as a father, he has done all these things. They are painful and embarrassing. These failures are the reason for the drink, the fumbling lifestyle, the sexual adventures he is damaged by. The way he lives with his failures is the reason he can't give up the notion that he must act competently, adequately, achievingly and so on and so forth.

It is not much to ask, he thinks, to live well, surely, it isn't too much to ask.

When things don't go the way she wants, she starts to believe that everything is awful. It's irrational, she knows that. But a black mist rises, the world goes dim, and her body fills with fear. It's all mental, and she should push the bad pictures away. She knows that. But do things ever go the way she wants? That man she met in the bar, that musician she picked up, did he have to turn out so unsatisfactory? He seemed so right, sitting there. All he needed was a woman's touch to bring him out of that awful sadness and back to the urbane, self-confident man he must have been before his . . . crisis. So . . . unsatisfactory. And so demanding, not like a man at all. More like a boy.

And then missing the flight. Two days late for the conference, now. No chance to catch up. All that money wasted. What would her father have thought of her? She was always so good at things. She had once been on top of things. When she was young and bright. Now look at her, drunk at thirty thousand feet, late again. She felt that everything — absolutely everything — was terrible, horrible, awful, and so on and so forth.

He knew that it would be better for him if he gave up the idea that certain people are bad, wicked or villainous and that they deserve severe blame or punishment. The way he purses his lips, you can tell what he's thinking. The way he frowns and shakes his head. The way his hands grip the balcony rail, the knuckles going white. He doesn't notice the boats, but we can see the boats on the water in the centre of the screen.

But Carol shouldn't have said that, he thinks. What right did she have to say that, the bitch? And why did she do those things? That was simply cruel. Not just to me — look what's happened to the boy. His little boy. Cruelty of that sort should be punished. She doesn't deserve to be happy. I deserve to be happy, after what I've gone through. She is bad, wicked, villainous, she deserves to be punished. Is that so unreasonable? Is that so unnatural, to feel like this?

At last he notices the boats, on the blue water. The television stammers in the room behind him, jerking from channel to channel, unattended.

She has gotten somewhere, she thinks. She has rid herself of the idea that human misery is externally caused, and that she has little or no ability to control her depression or self-pity. She has been there, she has gotten rid of that.

She has never tried to run away from life's difficulties and responsibilities. Well, responsibilities . . . she has run away from several personal relationships, to be honest, at some cost to herself and others. Is that true? She has another drink, enjoying the flavour. A drink in a plastic airlines cup. They will soon land in San Francisco, coming in from the south-east over Silicon Valley. She has a woman friend there, and the two of them will have a good time. She turns the thought over in her mind. Rehearsing the erotic possibilities. It is wrong to believe that the past remains all-important.

One more drink, she thinks to herself. She will be waiting for me. She turns that thought over slowly in her mind. Outside, the cloud, arranged in layers.

He is trying to give up the idea that people should be different from the way they are. It's just a thing he wants to do. Going back into the empty room. Pouring himself a glass of milk. Staring at the television at last.

On the screen an old man — very like his father, though with a stubble of beard — an old man is patiently explaining something to a young boy. The boy is sulking, and tugging at a chain. A small angry monkey is tugging at the other end. They are speaking Spanish.

He waits for the subtitles. Standing in the dimly-lit room, in his socks, holding a cigarette in one hand and a glass of cold milk in the other. The subtitles flash onto the screen, flicker, and disappear. They have said: 'Give up the idea, my boy, that life's problems can be solved quickly. After all, you have a lifetime ahead of you.'

He turns the television off. He turns out the light.

CALIFORNIAN POPPIES

The mothers of America created
a wave of television doctors just like
their fathers. Watched carefully by mothers
who were looking for faith, whose children
had left home and taken to the bad life.
Since then relationships with foreign girls
who study Art and English are only found in art;
and only cheap video shops stock them.

'I'd like to look at them as enrolments.'
That's a theoretical way for a girl like you
to wrestle your soft options to the ground —
give me more practical examples.
'From my personal experience of advertising
I can wrestle successfully with women;
that's something, isn't it?'

Many years later she became the career editor
of one of his really conservative manuscripts,
standing up for the red light against radicals —
'Be old-fashioned, for good epic poets
are a delight to read, young pup.'
And her job was consuming manuscripts
written on some new edible paper.
'Take this typescript, it's depressing —
you're not an academic, are you, Betty?'

I'll talk about what I know: Oh, Helen!
I've had an ambiguous collapse to the extent
that everything went dark for a long time.
It is strange, and rather dark. (In a way
we think it's always a dark time, though
to me it seems there are dual personalities
and I don't care for either of you.)

It's true that friction's good for energy, e.g.
a wheel spinning, but not us silly billies
fighting: epic, romantic or alliterative.

His father's nightmare: an axeman attacked
by a mad Golem, another axeman, so he
fears an old tradition of axing relatives.
The same school he feared, and never mentioned,
was easier for me to talk about — talk?
real men's talk? — do they want that, the women?
'The love of women is the decorative inconceivable,'
he says, 'for when I was a teenager I dreamed
pulp novels, usually fervid, often lewd, and
when the burst of hard work ended
I thought I was quite grown up.' What a
cynical Australian I am — oh, go on —

a Master of the Martial Arts, in a red kimono,
produces a book from his sleeve
singed by the flame of wisdom, and lets
a gentleman emptying the jars of flowers
explain how his philosophy of 'God the Gentleman'
can save you. But nobody's listening.
So he brings in the Sicilian exemplars.

Out there behind the blocks of vacant land
in the back seat of his limousine, she gulps
whisky, remembering her sartorial accident
and the wise, beautifully-groomed doctors
who attended her — her torn clothes — and the way
her mother smiled at the doctors — O Hippocrates —
Oh, shame!
              'The apostrophe they invented
was easy to understand,' and both his parents
were torn between two kinds of language,
between Baroque, and something Second-Generation,

at its most complex and powerful up at the University
of Discoworld. In a critical domain intended
to facilitate an all-out attack on the culture
the rack of cheap suits exemplified, he heard
that somebody was dying to kiss him.

Hurry up, Doodle-Bug! The clock represents
inevitable disease — he runs back to his early
art conflict, where Sex, Death, and Lots of Money
whirl into a maelstrom of instruction,
teaching him how to fight, how to fail,
how to emerge from the tricks of language
into the love-glare that awaited him.

SAIL AWAY

1.

Angel, strip away the coloured
future from the rag trade baby
dreamers and their preppy jazz
aboard the Cruise Bay Bomber.

Her glass of chloral hydrate spills,
herself the airport and calculator —
the moving arm writes out a secret
digit whispered in a hollow
auditorium or an underwater cave —

diving and deep breathing, it gives me
a belief in endless life — up above
I pump the tank full of hissy gas
then repaint baby's lipstick, the
speeding clouds — pucker up —
reflected in the soft coral red
gloss like a whirlpool

kiss kiss I'm gone

I'll ask that young typist number
out tonight, with the dreamy green
eyes: her hands are quite small,

each touch a magic answer to your
precise misery status, a massage so
gentle it hardly touches your skin,

lighter than a breeze your face feels
on the merry-go-round helix, your rear-
vision mirror full of parked trucks or
their double images, the country girls
shooting at jerky ducks and laughing

when the bullet hits the bell so
their cowboy guys get embarrassed.

I laze on the Sydney beaches
like a tourist, it's almost
tropical — this blurring in a
wine bar retracking as the steam
fractures the glass then clears
the view, starred quartz:

because you bossed her she's sobbing
as the sophomores taught her, her
hand hesitant that recently
stroked the keyboard or belted out
arguments. The movie reconstructs
Dad's car, the gang, the high school;

and I learn to say goodbye to half
my life, goodbye to rock'n'roll —
in middle age, my teenage tears
blurring the radio dial — I
was a kid, a different music,
different girl, et cetera.

A cracking sound, and the rain
gets heavier for a while then the
rest arrives, disguised as a trunk,
a whistle, a hollow, a violent slap,

a lock, a paradoxical question; in the
trash-can sticky Airfix glue patching
a background of brightness, and the
thirst that reaches out to harrow,

curtains of pink and yellow crepe
backgrounding the clock and the announcer

it seems pointless to question getting
fucked around by women — a fit of weakness.

Daffodils in a bowl, some fruit punch
after she'd swept the room, I'm not a
kid — I know how to back up, when they
hurt; the Mormon touch, the fairer sex.

My heart impaled on the rough end
of a love affair; a digit more to
the Devil's Accountant — Oh Christ,
I could really fall in love again,

with that one: what is it? Her skin?
Her gaze like a tunnel of love?
If I could do it, her room would be
full of florists, falling over each
other, no more misery — growing up,

I'm sick of it, the heart pumping . . .
the way the man deals the good luck
cards I can kiss my career goodbye.

You lack that splint gift to patch up
the breaks, but we can fix it, okay?
One or two stiff drinks with a chick
at closing time. My last wife — for
all her violence she taught me things:

a tougher bargainer's emerging:
watch me knock out the trade-wind
dreamers with the toss of a coin.

There's always fun for a bright kid,
no stress fractures unless the women
are really foolish and fall in love.

That pool of sentiment! Their bones
moving spell out a magic number.

And heavy breathing under the
yellow moon, it's the teenagers
dreaming of the perfect linkage.

Notice how the heat rebuilds the
suffering here in the suburbs,
despite the Serepax, the wives
rehearsing a role each, crying
at the dishwasher, saving time —

no more weeping under the washing
line, is that good for the family?
To suffer love wounds and the kids
always leaving, they learn it quick.

His hands cruel I was just a kid
with a different man, and so forth.

There are motels,
                        yes, in the suburbs.

A tearing sound, it makes bad
luck, a parcel, a promise broken,
a tragic love puzzle your dreaming
takes ages to answer: forty years
of cupboard drinking at home — or

drinking at the Leagues Club Friday
night the bar shifting and stranding you
sad and plump in front of the mirrors
in the fun-house just as the hot gas
fractures the glass.
                        You're an artist,

how do you represent the view that
means so much to you without painting
it in a clumsy gesture as though
grunting 'Here, look!' Your girl-
friend's dress ballooning over the
blast canopy as the movies taught
her, playing cute for the lady
photographer, who lately scribbled
the mechanics exam or struggled with
politics. Oh Jesus I'd do just about
anything to get married! How the petrol

haze half-hid the sixties, you learn
it, vaguely, uh, he remembers, mmm,
answering his touch when I was
a kid in a different motel room,

a different man, more or less. A
smacking sound, and the light
gets dimmer for a moment.
                              How long

it takes for the promise to arrive,
shaped as a flirt, a cheating
kiss, a whistle, an ambulance.

2.

No regrets, she's aboard
the cruiser reaching the open
sea at last herself the course
calculator the screen only prints
digits. The streets close down
a huge listener how she spells
and calculates goodbye a pink

lipstick each pale green wave
kisses watching your breath
or give back paradise reached
only by boat, mouth against
yours, puff hard the gas into
your mouth breathing hot you
ask that number tonight, yes
do it, valuable dark eyes.

Her hands perfect, small, each
magic number flair breaking
for love in parked cars, or
their own images in front of
them on the screen displaying
the glare of Australia flash
or dressed for a cooler — no,
more temperate climate. The
radar retracking vapour mists
the glass, and you float
clear of the beach starry-
eyed fool love dreamer my
childhood slowly ending with
celebrations I don't fully
understand the grotesque garb
the girlish priests wear black.

Heat ripples precisely re-
making the mirror images,
you break it, forgetting her
fun parlour hopes, a kid
out of her depth with those
bastards in different rooms,
men begging pain the light
flickers briefly. Ah, the rest
will arrive, shaped now as a
track, a howl, a bristle, a

tiny horror, sleep, the blood
gently counting the wrist to
kiss that bunch of dolls — boy,

was I fucked over by those dames —
won't you answer? Was he always
neurotic, they ask, look these
parallel damages, happening
after he'd been taken to the
hospital and I'm not a kid — I
know they hurt; the adults touching
the private parts tenderly. Would
you be skewered on the flowers —
the flowers, fortunate, misery,
medical enjoyment — I'm sick,
watery vision . . . my lack, that
power gift adoration and for
cruelty he broke me in two:

a stronger person plotting
a drench of blue is how you
sucker the rich Baby Boomers
voyaging for fun and profit a
woman raises the metal harness
the money-changers laughing —

now they spell out the city:
its giant drug parks, the street
deals kiss my nostrils and that
scented darkness breathing,
give me back the sun, the
heat remakes the blisters here
or in the suburbs, can it be done?

My old school falling down re-
member it, please, how when I

was a kid with a different
older woman, or a man, after,
that too, too many, after, and
so breaking, a breaking sound,
it takes for the rest crying
to drive there, and park, whose
motel I don't know, should I?

Always wanting more love her
lonely dreaming in the South
Land neolithic technology that
steel trolley the brick ramp,
the truck, drinking poison
as the way out, home, alcohol
retracking the vapour plumes
the window view fracturing

now beg you my ill-starred
voyager second-hand car by
moonlight your style throwaway
an older woman learning too much
as the teenagers taught her,
that recently learned it,
the love trick, her plump body
adolescent in a different
room, the fifties, a smacking
sound, and the light glows
softly for a moment.

How long it takes for
the rest to arrive,
shaped as a kiss, a
cuddle, a child.

HALOTHANE

The angel loves the lake trip stripping off
you too writhing under the heap of women
loose now only within their roles,
their manacles: 'wives'. Embrace me
hotly it's a childish trick from that
ink-black cloud a string conducting
death shocks we have the key to,
sweeping the grass drenched and happy
with promises in the academics of passion;
her touch brings a thrill of hurt
as much as delirium, pleasure
and a feast of busy dresses,
the shopgirls dizzy with
        fever for her.

At dawn a flame breaks from the edge of rain
and I'm clutching at you, accumulating merit
under the mandarin tree, then from her torn
frock her tits burst firm and heavy on the
thick grass, teaching him gentleness
as much as astronomy, the holy stellar Dance.
But if I fuck you, the lovely young woman
says to the other, my life
becomes mechanical and shameful,
the planets tumble out of their courses —
        and how can we marry?

Blizzard discourse
with a giant submerged author
in the bottom of a suitcase
you faint in a corner: one trick,
two tricks. Oh, go on, he hears
the swing windows open out of focus
and he trips through a glass door
sweating yet cool as ice — then a
hotly-coloured, more balanced switching-off.

The young woman has a flashgun trained
on her future, but the wet circuit fails
and so a blurred vision of the past
blocks her struggle to be new, a guy
in a convertible with a handgun —
        is that her husband?

The cathode screen dim aquarium
ghost of speech rehearses rhyme
among the nurses and the night-light
orange glow across the empty cave —
the weapons fixed, enough pressure
getting women to explore the surface
even if they're bombed the sound of a
lack danger manual he realises the lack
the damage is happening now he
overhears murmuring and sees the gloves
and the blue plastic blood bags,
his pet nurses move functionally
designed to kill pain on the table
like meat under the knife he assumes
his eager uptown firearm grin
the dying republics and their legends
parade before us urgent oxygen faith
leads out from our nervous gestures
to the air pump and her green gloves
as the agony moves away the studio
lights explode slow motion launch
burst through the broken floor
panels hissing gas the needle
the halothane the blue tablet
and plead with the Admiral of Water
        to carry you home.

The way of the Gold Flash
both kids eager to operate together —
reading 'go' he fumbles up to the horizon.
The ice in my gaze flashes back —
fun in the back seat paying off the woman
for the play that exhilarates
picked up on sheets of radar green.
To romp among the fields of this casual
love she writes a pornographic novel
in her room inscribed in Hotel Italian,
you say 'no' but you secretly wanted
that brief brutal meeting
        then forgiveness.

His X-Ray vision sees the suburbs
rich with hidden graves:
rusting police cars grind across a field
under a wall of rain and thunder
and the muzak takes you home —
giant shocks lift you through the ceiling —
this is the end of the line.
This dream in L.A. International:
through tinted glass the tropics,
then the wipers, then the horrors of Europe
reeled across the screen: sleet, bad sex,
the firing squad, how do you measure it?
Endless inventions waiting with your enemies
at the restaurant no one knows about —
another man's name inked on the
marriage certificate — your roles
were being shuffled in the house of shame,
your hurt rain and ruin all your misery
slipping back to your death but your
gift of love can change history, and cover
        the dark with radiance.

The affair's beginning he speaks
as though it's almost a craft:
kindness rationed out among the ruins,
loving in the gift of flesh repeats
the call of the wild whispered
the alcohol burners fanning lust
into a wise terrible flame. Knocked out
in the hold and murmuring in his sleep
	the Captain will explain

how dozing under a rainy sky looking upwards
you see the clouds trapped in huge circling
tunnels of air the girl with golden hair sways
under the tilting sky you're in love and it
	goes on forever

FOUR EPIGRAMS

THE LATIN MOTTO

Sporting a lurex T-shirt
and a spiked haircut several
years too young for him
    the ageing artist

told me he'd given up dope.
Hungover, paranoid, he quoted
the motto 'A healthy mind
    in a healthy body.'

This, while jogging on the spot
among the flash, the trendy and
the unemployed, on fashionable
    Bondi Beach.

UNIFORM

When the middle-aged poet's name
came up, Winston put him down —
'Oh, him — he's the kind of guy who
irons his jeans!' Boy, what a knockout!

Winston's a youngish poet, does drugs,
looks laid-back, but very acute —
the kind of guy who says 'Oh, him —
he's the kind of guy who irons his jeans!'

CICADA GAMBIT

Exiled by circumstance and inclination
from the land and language of his childhood
and deprived by fate of half his family,
he settled uneasily in his father's landscape.
    From the blue Aegean

he declined to Darlinghurst, exchanging the dialect
of Callimachus and Cavafy for the meat-pie-eaters'
drab vernacular. For this indignity, a gentleman's
revenge: he wrought the vulgar tongue into
    exquisite poetry.

ALEXANDRIA

Bring a cold bottle from the fridge
to the corner table, in the sun —
there, you can see the Harbour Bridge.

And Apollonius the Librarian
said he was a happy man when
his silly *Argonautica* was done.

NOTES

'I have just written a . . . poem, but I do not quite know what it means, and I have come to see you that you should explain it to me.' (Mallarmé, to a friend, according to Joseph Bard, *Transactions of the Royal Society of Literature*, vol. xxvi, Introduction, p.vi; quoted in John Press, *The Chequer'd Shade*, Oxford University Press, London, 1963, p.93.)

p.4   **The Pool**
'the poet Apollonius' — Apollonius Rhodius (about 280—215 B.C.) was a scholar in the great library at Alexandria. His epic poem *Argonautica* retells the voyages of Jason and the Argonauts. See the note on the poem 'Alexandria', below.

p.7   **The Bedroom Mirrors, 2**
'photographs / were flopped' — when a photographic negative is placed wrong-side up and exposed onto a printing plate, the subsequent printed image appears reversed left-to-right, or 'flopped'.

p.23   **The Guides**
Robinson's and Gregory's street directories/atlases compete for the patronage of the Sydney driver.

p.28   **Cruising Height**
'petrol-scented dawn' — unlike *rhododactylos* (see note on 'On Looking Into The American Anthology') the epithet *petrelaiosmos* ('petrol-scented') is rare in ancient Greek. It may be connected with an early form of 'Greek Fire', though the apparent prochronism makes this unlikely. The Dutch scholar Winckelschnippe renders a papyrus fragment as follows (noting its probable derivation from Call. *Epigr.* xlvii, and reading 'Eros' as 'Cupid'):

WHAT THE CYCLOPS SAID

> . . . poets have (two?) remedies
> against Love's engineer — Hunger,
> that lives in their pockets, and
> (their own) (intoxicating?) Muse.
>
> So, Cupid, petrol-scented boy,
> (back to) your chariots . . .
> . . . your business with axle-grease!
> We have a double remedy against you!

p.31 **The Creature from the Black Lagoon**
Originally filmed in 3-D, this 1954 movie was directed by Jack Arnold.
See 'High School Confidential' below.

'yellow / foreigner' — cowardly, not coloured.

'like a dead / king' — William Shakespeare, *Hamlet,* Act V, Scene i,
Lines 210-216:

> *Hamlet:* . . . Alexander died, Alexander was buried,
>   Alexander returneth to dust; the dust is earth; of
> earth we make loam; and why of that loam whereto he was
> converted might they not stop a beer barrel?
>   Imperious Caesar, dead and turned to clay,
>   Might stop a hole to keep the wind away.

p.33 **High School Confidential**
This 1958 monochrome rock'n'roll movie was directed by Jack Arnold,
who also directed 'The Creature from the Black Lagoon'.

p.34 **Stratocruiser**
A lumbering giant in its time, and biggest of the immediately post-war
transports, the Boeing 377 Stratocruiser was derived from the B-29
bomber. It had four 3,500 hp engines and two pressurised decks seating
up to 100 on transatlantic routes. Only 55 civil examples were sold and
the type is chiefly remembered because it usually had a downstairs bar.

p.38 **Letter to America, 3**
'NORAD' — North American Air Defence Command, a vast radar
nerve centre and attack control post operated by Canada and the
United States of America. As a protection against nuclear attack, the
Command Operations Center of NORAD is buried some 1,200 to
1,750 feet below the top of 9,565-foot Cheyenne Mountain, in the
Rampart Range of the Rocky Mountains, seven miles south-west of
Colorado Springs. It was opened in April, 1966. World War Three
begins on the screens and control panels of NORAD.

p.40 **On Looking Into The American Anthology**
'rhododactylos' — 'rosy-fingered', a common epithet for the dawn in
ancient Greek verse. Both Homer and Sappho used the stock phrase.

p.42 **Laminex**
'Persian Room' — haunt of the poet August Kleinzahler, transported to
Sydney for the purposes of this poem from its usual location in back of
Bruno Mooshei's Persian Aub Zam Zam Room bar in the Haight
district, San Francisco.

p.43　**Having Completed My Fortieth Year**
The poem is a stanza-by-stanza reply to Peter Porter's poem 'On This Day I Complete My Fortieth Year', which was brought to my attention by Richard Connolly on the occasion of my fortieth birthday.

'drudger's barge' — see immediately below.

'being "absolutely modern" as my mentor taught' — Arthur Rimbaud (1854—91) is responsible for the phrase 'one must be absolutely modern' *('Il faut etre absolument moderne.')* He stopped writing at the age of approximately twenty. A dredger's barge appears in his poem 'Memory' as follows (in Oliver Bernard's admirable prose translation): '. . . the breath of the poplars above is all there is for a breeze. Then it is the sheet of water without reflections and without a spring, grey: an old man, a dredger, in his motionless boat, labours.'

'twin cities' — London and New York, seen from Sydney, Australia, and vice versa.

p.46　**Lufthansa**
The poem reconstructs a flight from Venice to Munich.

'the north side / of the woods and model villages' — in the northern hemisphere in spring the sun melts the snow lying on the south side of large objects (buildings and hedges, for example) leaving a shadow-print of unmelted snow on their northern side; a sight best appreciated from above.

p.51　**Those Gods Made Permanent**
'the old Remington' — the typewriter, not the repeating rifle.

Among the movies referred to are Fritz Lang's 'Doktor Mabuse' and Joseph Losey's 'The Servant'.

p.68　**Papyrus**
Ezra Pound's poem 'Papyrus', a translation of the fragmentary remains of the first three lines of a (much longer) poem by Sappho, is discussed in Hugh Kenner's *The Pound Era*. It was reconstructed from a fragment of papyrus that came to Berlin from Egypt in 1896. Pound's poem runs as follows:

> Spring . . . .
> Too long . . . .
> Gongula . . . .

'hetaerae' — 'As the law forbade the marriage of Athenian citizens except with the daughters of other Athenian citizens, a sort of irregular union with foreign women was frequent in the 5th and 4th centuries B.C. These women, known as *hetaerae* (. . . literally 'companions', and including concubines and courtesans), were often Ionians, whose charm was increased by a high degree of intelligence and education, making them more agreeable companions than the cloistered Athenian women.' *(The Oxford Companion to Classical Literature.)*

p.73 **Spin-the-Bottle**
'Mister President' — because of the mispronunciation of Herbert Hoover's name by a functionary, it has since been traditional never to use the personal name of the President of the United States at any public occasion. He is always referred to as 'Mister President'.

p.75 **Crosstalk**
'Crosstalk' — when a signal from one channel is audible in the other, for example, in a stereo tape recording.

p.76 **At The Newcastle**
'The Newcastle' — Jim Buckley's Newcastle Hotel, in George Street near Circular Quay in Sydney, was during the 60s the legendary watering-hole of a mix of journalists, writers, painters and philosophers. It has been apotheosised in Martin Johnston's novel *Cicada Gambit*. It has since been demolished.

'idiot box' — slang, for television receiver.

p.82 **Trolley**
'Ducking for Apples' — otherwise known as 'Bobbing for Apples', a party game where the participant has to take a floating apple from a tub of water using only his or her teeth. Dorothy Parker is supposed to have walked into a party and asked her host 'What are they doing?' 'Why, ducking for apples,' he replied. Parker sighed and said 'There, but for a typographical error, is the story of my life.'

p.84 **Dirty Weekend**
'fuck-truck' — a ranch wagon, station wagon or panel van fitted out with a mattress. For its emergence through Australian slang into poetry, see Professor Gerald Wilkes, *Dictionary of Australian Colloquialisms*, 1985 edition.

p.88 **La Pulqueria**
'La Pulqueria' — a *pulqueria* is a Mexican bar selling *pulque*, a milky brew derived from the agave.

p.90 **The Subtitles**
A fuller and more reasonable treatment of the ten delusory beliefs that feature in this piece can be found in Albert Ellis and Robert Harper, *A New Guide To Rational Living*.

p.100 **Sail Away**
'chloral hydrate' — a sleeping draught, and the chief ingredient of the 'Micky Finn' knockout cocktail.

p.108 **Halothane**
'halothane' — a volatile, sweetish liquid, $Cf_3CHBrCl$, used as an anaesthetic inhalant.

p.113 **Cicada Gambit**
The poet Martin Johnston's novel *Cicada Gambit* was published by Hale & Iremonger, Sydney, in 1983. Martin Johnston was born in Sydney, spent his childhood in Greece, and returned to Australia with his parents, the writers George Johnston and Charmian Clift, in the 1960s. Currently he lives in Darlinghurst, a Sydney suburb with views of the Harbour.

'Callimachus' — (born in Cyrene, about 310 B.C.) was a scholar-librarian, and a poet of the Alexandrian school. See note below.

p.113 **Alexandria**
Like Sydney, Alexandria was a polyglot mercantile city-port founded as a colony and situated far from the great centres of empire in classical times, Athens and Rome. The diaspora of Greek writing from the centre to the periphery is instructive. According to *The Oxford Companion to Classical Literature*, during the 5th and 4th centuries B.C., 25 authors were born in Greece proper, and twelve (mainly philosophers) in Sicily and in other Greek colonies. After 300 B.C., during the Hellenistic, Roman and Byzantine ages, only five authors were born in Greece proper, while some 24 were born in the colonies. Callimachus (see note above) was the quintessential Alexandrian poet. Apollonius Rhodius (see note on 'The Pool' above) was at one time his pupil. Callimachus favoured poetic forms such as the epigram (at which he excelled) because of their brevity. Indeed, in the Loeb Classical Library edition of his epigrams, some of the footnotes are considerably longer than the poems they adumbrate. Though he was the most admired and the most imitated poet in antiquity among the later Romans, the liking for brief poems in apparently simple diction that require extensive exegesis eventually declined; a fact for which the modern reader can be thankful. Apollonius argued on the other hand for the epic; his long poem *Argonautica* (in four books) is exemplary. The quarrel between Callimachus and his erstwhile pupil on this issue apparently became a bitter one, and it is thought that because of it Apollonius was obliged to leave Alexandria and languish for some time on the island of Rhodes, where he was given the freedom of the city (and the appellation 'Rhodius'). Legend has it they were reconciled, and were buried alongside one another in the grounds of the great Library at Alexandria where they had both worked.

More UQP POETRY

Thomas Shapcott *Welcome!*
Dimitris Tsaloumas *The Observatory*
Evan Jones *Left at the Post*
Philip Mead *This River is in the South*
Gary Catalano *Slow Tennis*
Cornelis Vleeskens *The Day The River*
John Blight *Holiday Sea Sonnets*
John A. Scott *St Clair*
Andrew Taylor *Travelling*
Dimitris Tsaloumas *The Book of Epigrams*
Richard Kelly Tipping *Nearer by Far*
Lewis Packer *Serpentine Futures*
Silvana Gardner *The Devil in Nature*
Michael Sariban *A Formula for Glass*
Thomas Shapcott *Travel Dice*
Susan Afterman *Rain*
Thomas Shapcott *Shabbytown Calendar*
Gary Catalano *Fresh Linen*
Dimitris Tsaloumas *Falcon Drinking*